OFF TH

A Perspective on Athletic Coaching

CURTIS W. TONG

 Areté Press, 480 West Sixth Street, Claremont, CA 91711

© 1991, Areté Press, 480 West Sixth Street, Claremont, CA 91711
All rights reserved.

ISBN 0-941736-04-0

TABLE OF CONTENTS

1	COACHING PHILOSOPHY	1
2	FAMILY	7
3	FAITH	13
4	RESPONSIBILITY	19
5	LIKEABLE IMAGE	25
6	DEVELOPING CONFIDENCE	33
7	INNOVATION	39
8	LISTENING	45
9	DEALING WITH ADVERSITY	51
10	FOREIGN TRAVEL	55
11	CHANGING JOBS	61
12	LEADERSHIP	65
13	RECRUITING	73
14	PROGRAM PROMOTION	83
15	COMMUNICATION	89
16	DISCIPLINE	95
17	SPORTSMANSHIP	103
18	CREATING A MORAL SENSE	107
19	EMOTION	115
20	SUBSTANCE ABUSE	123
21	SEXISM	131
22	RACISM	141
23	THE TEACHING OF VALUES	149

Acknowledgements

The author would like to thank the following people:

Ronald Rubin and Susan Perry, for editorial assistance in the preparation of the manuscript.

Jinx Tong and our children Karinne Heise, Kyle Tong, and Kurt Tong, for their moral support and forthright suggestions.

Diana Wilson, for assistance in the computerization and organization of the manuscript.

Dr. Yoshio Niwa, Dr. Sean Sloane, Dr. Robert Peck, Dr. Thomas Kerr, Mr. Jack Mehl, Mr. James Westhall, and Mr. Anthony Yates, for their friendship and support.

Mrs. Walter C. Tong, for her eternal excitement over the completion of this book.

Those coaches, both overseas and at home, with whom I have worked and against whom I have competed, for their selfless sharing of ideas and knowledge.

The hundreds of young men and women who have touched my life through coaching at Bexley High School, Otterbein College, University of Vermont, Williams College, and the Pomona-Pitzer Colleges.

1
COACHING PHILOSOPHY
a base for decision making

> The philosophy which is so important in each of us is not a technical matter; it is our more or less dumb sense of what life honestly and deeply means. It is only partly got from books; it is our individual way of just seeing and feeling the total push and pressure of the cosmos.
> *Pragmatism*, William James

One way to judge coaches is by their records — the number of champions they have developed or the number of championships their teams have won. In many educational settings, however, coaches are appreciated as much for their contribution to the personal growth of the young people in their charge as for the number of wins they log. And the coaches who are most effective in their endeavors with young people are those most at peace with themselves. These coaches achieve most because their actions answer to a dictating philosophy. Philosophy is therefore a vital base important to successful coaching.

Coaches, like any other human beings, are living, breathing, playing, praying, thinking people. Coaches are also social people who constantly touch the lives of administrators, fans, parents, spouses, reporters, students, players, and other coaches. Through all these contacts, through all these relationships, a single thread must pass, like a string through a beaded necklace: the coach must have a philosophy for guidance. Successful coaching therefore rests on a philosophical base — a source of power from which the coach draws, consciously or subconsciously, in the course of all decision-making.

Imagine a coach who takes one line on a certain issue when talking to reporters, another when talking to parents, and yet another when talking to players. Or imagine a coach who sets moral guidelines for players and then violates those guidelines in the conduct of his or her own life. Such inconsistency diminishes respect and distances the coach from some constituency. The way for coaches to avoid such inconsistency is to develop a philosophy suited to them.

Philosophy and Self-knowledge

Bobby Knight, the fiery coach of Indiana's basketball team, has often been criticized for tactless vulgarity, for having a short fuse, and for his "General Patton" approach to practice sessions. Yet most coaches respect Knight because his philosophy is consistent and because it fits him. Knight doesn't reserve his vulgarity for reporters, his fuse is short with many, and he doesn't hide the nature of his practice sessions. One always knows where Knight stands. He has a deep-rooted philosophy and he stands by it. Over time, his philosophy has come to fit him like a worn pair of shoes.

A philosophy is an extension of a coach's personality — a "guidance system" for the coach's work. At the foundation of every successful coaching career I have seen rests a coaching philosophy that reflects the coach's understanding of self. And almost every coaching career I have seen go asunder lacked this philosophical base.

In Herb Gardner's *A Thousand Clowns*, which is one of my favorite movies, a character named Arnold, happy with himself and the material comforts of his world, admonishes his brother Murray, who rebels against the hypocrisies of American society:

> I have long been aware, Murray, that you don't respect me much....Unfortunately for you, Murray, you want to be a hero....There are people who spill things and people who get spilled on. I chose not to notice the stains....You cannot convince me that I am one of the bad guys. I get up....I lie a little, I peddle a little....I talk the talk....I can catch the wind and go with it however it blows. But...I am the best possible Arnold Burns.

If he had little else, Arnold had a good understanding of himself.

Coaches should understand themselves too. What they believe about coaching, what they do in their relationships with athletes, what they do in their private and professional lives, their very philosophies of coaching and living depend on the knowledge they have of themselves.

At the conclusion of one of my coaching classes, a student asked the guest lecturer, a prominent midwestern football coach, to name the one point he found most important in his own career — the one bit of advice he would give to students preparing for the coaching profession. His simple reply: "Be yourself."

Delbert Oberteuffer, long the resident sage in Physical Education at Ohio State University, once offered me similar advice. "If you want to have impact in your profession," Oberteuffer told me, "discover yourself and be yourself."

This is good advice. Each of us is a unique being, beautiful in that uniqueness. The ability to recognize that beauty, believe in its existence, love it, and share it so that others recognize it and respect it is a key to coaching effectiveness.

During the glory days of Ohio State football, Coach Woody Hayes was famous in most Ohio communities, and he was viewed as a messiah in the city of Columbus. Small wonder that budding football coaches took to wearing baseball caps and short-sleeved white shirts as Hayes did. One junior high school coach — a young, almost shy former college football player — carried the "Hayes style" a step farther: he cuffed his charges on the sides of their helmets after they made mistakes and benched players for the duration of a game if they fumbled, as he had seen Hayes do at Ohio Stadium. The shortness of his coaching career should not come as a surprise. His error was failing to see that he was *not* Woody Hayes. The volatile Hayes could be accepted as a tough drill-sergeant, but his hard-line of coaching did not fit this young coach and people did not respect him for it.

On a similar note, I vividly recall my first game as a college basketball coach. The game was played at a rival university whose excellent team included two Little All-Americans. Our starting line-up was composed of five young men cumulatively having had only one previous game of college experience. Pessimism hung over the team in pre-game warm-ups. And at halftime, my shell-shocked, embarrassed team scurried to the locker room trailing by 25 points. For some reason, probably having to do with my newness to the college game, I delivered half-time encouragement to my intimidated troops in gentle whispers.

As I spoke, I saw Tony Yates standing by the locker room door. Yates had been a stalwart during my tenure as coach for the armed services' Strategic Air Command squad, and he was later an All-American and captain of the national champion Cincinnati Bearcats. Yates said nothing as I whispered to my team, of course. But, when the team had exited the locker room to return to the floor, he asked if he could make a suggestion. He was known in Cincinnati as "Mr. Defense," and I thought his remarks might be about defensive tactics. But what Yates said was this: "That didn't sound like *you* talking to them at halftime."

Yates was right. With the military team, it had not been my habit to whisper gentle niceties at halftime. Rather it had been my practice to find some facet of their play during the first half of a game about which to raise my voice; I had always made a point to reflect my caring through more than hushed tones. Yates' comments were a strong reminder to me to recognize my natural coaching manner. Never again during my coaching life have I allowed myself to forget his advice.

For some the raised voice is not natural or effective. An example is Dick Price, who coached football at a small, private academy in the midwest. Price has my greatest respect, and his teams were legendary. Yet Price rarely raised his voice. He coached with quiet affability. Sometimes, on hot days, he would call off practice sessions and drive his team to a nearby lake for an afternoon of swimming and sailing. He adhered to a "no cut" policy. In his program, everyone dressed for the game and everyone played. And his record was unparalleled for many years. He succeeded because he knew himself, applied his personality to his coaching, and sold that personality to his students.

It isn't always easy to be oneself. Coaches sometimes feel cornered, flustered, and fearful. They find themselves saying and doing things that are not really them. They ask "What's happening to me?", "What am I doing?", and even "Who am I?" In their panic, they become confused — because they haven't really thought through who they really are, what they really believe, what their goals are, and how they hope to achieve those goals. In other words, their philosophies are not sufficiently grounded or suitably defined. They have nowhere to turn for solutions to their problems.

Critical to the development of a coaching philosophy are peer appraisal, instructor appraisal, and self-appraisal. The experience of "bouncing oneself" off people who know us best (peers) and people who have measured our educational progress (instructors) leads to objectivity in assessment of philosophical readiness. But most important is self-appraisal — the "mirror experience" of looking at oneself and into oneself.

William James wrote,

> Not that I would not, if I could, be both handsome and fat, and well-dressed and a great athlete, and make a million a year, be a wit, and a lady-killer, a philanthropist, a statesman...and a saint. But the thing is simply impossible.

James was right; we have to make choices about who we will be. And the choices should fit us like pieces of apparel. Before we choose, we need to know exactly who we are. We need to take responsibility for who and where we are rather than blaming others or our circumstances.

Doing this is like waking up, gazing in a mirror, recognizing ourselves, and being proud of what we see. It's like moving from illusion to truth. It's like unmasking ourselves and dealing with all our blemishes.

Often coaches have an impact on young peoples' lives greater than parents or other teachers. When the impact is favorable, it is not just due to coaches' recognition of their flaws, but to their understanding of their own uniqueness and their ability to share this understanding with the players on their teams. Only with a full knowledge of themselves can they enter fully into each day's coaching labors, affect each athlete positively, and achieve fulfillment as coaches.

Patience in the Development of Philosophy

The adage "It takes several years for concrete to solidify" has its application to the profession of coaching. The philosophy essential to coaching cannot be developed overnight but must come slowly as the product of education, experience, and self-understanding.

I recall two former students who took different approaches to the development of coaching philosophies. Each had been an excellent collegiate basketball player, each decided on coaching as a career, and each was courted by several school districts. But the similarity ended there. One chose without hesitation to be a head basketball coach at a middle-sized high school. The other, after days of agonizing indecision, became an assistant coach at a large secondary school. The first felt fully prepared for the rigors of professional coaching, but the other felt he needed more time to develop a secure philosophical base.

Two years later, the one who had chosen the job as head coach abandoned the profession with his self-confidence reeling, bitter and disillusioned. But, after twenty fulfilling years, the other one continues to coach, now as head coach, in the community where he began his career. Despite his lackluster won/lost record, he is revered, and one wing of a planned sports facility will be named in his honor.

What explains the difference? The one who initially chose the job of assistant coach temporarily avoided the pressures that head coaches face, and he therefore had time to observe, time to listen, time to reflect, time to mold his thoughts into a philosophy that suited him. The other did not take time to develop philosophical maturation. I think that this is why the one coaching career succeeded while the other failed.

It takes time to learn how to be an effective coach, and the time spent in preparing for a job in coaching is extremely important for success. The foundation for a successful career in coaching is a coaching philosophy, and the failure to take the time to develop such a philosophy often causes disillusionment and consternation later on.

The Place of Victory in Coaching Philosophy

In a sound coaching philosophy, victory is viewed as a means, not as an end.

Dana Bible, a former professor and football coach of national fame, suggested that nothing is more important in sports than that young men and women continually learn from their experiences in them. In particular, said Bible, young people should learn these things from sports

> to control and command their own powers; to focus them upon a single goal; to mobilize them quickly and completely; to think fast and realistically; to disregard pain and risk in pursuit of a desired end; to subordinate their interests to the interests of the group; to coordinate their activity with the activity of others engaged in the same task; to call up and expend in an emergency their last reserves of strength and courage; to pour out all their energies in a furious effort, observing at the same time a chivalrous regard for the rights of others, the rules of the game, and the limits dictated by decency and sportsmanship.

In my opinion, an institutional coach who tries to attain even some of these goals for each student will make giant strides toward a purposeful career in coaching.

To reach these goals, however, coaches must demand much of themselves and their teams. There must be no talk suggesting a lack of concern for victory. We must try to make games exciting exhibitions of skill, daring, and technique. We must strive for victory, work hard for it.

Yet, in our effort to win, we must never forget that victory is a means and not an end, that our basic purpose is to help young people grow into decent, kind, and sound men and women.

No coach can truthfully say that his or her coaching philosophy has consistently produced athletes who can serve as models for society. But coaches can at least hope that some who have come under their influence have received sparks that will light fires for society's betterment.

2
FAMILY
a source of support

Nobody who has not been in the interior of a family can say what the difficulties of any individual of that family may be.

Jane Austen, *Emma*

Billy Tubbs, resourceful basketball coach of Oklahoma University, has commented on the problem of coaches' family relationships. When Tubbs' wife suggested that he loved basketball more than he loved her, he quipped back, "Well, I love you more than *track*."

Most of the married coaches I know have experienced some strain in their family relationships. In fact, many say that the absence of normal family experiences is one of the major drawbacks to their profession. Many able sports leaders find their way into less demanding occupations after a few years in the coaching profession and many others, feeling married to their jobs rather than their spouses, end up in divorce courts. In this chapter, I will describe some of the problems faced by married coaches and suggest some solutions.

Problems

During the early years of my own collegiate coaching, I gained the knowledge that an unjust imbalance existed between the time and attention I gave to my coaching responsibilities and that devoted to my family. I was jolted into seeing this imbalance when, while readying the infield for a baseball game, I learned of the birth of my second child. I simply was inaccessible to my wife at a time when she most needed me. Later, in a three week stretch during a particularly grueling basketball season, I did not see my children at all except when I peeked into their bedrooms in the middle of the night to glimpse at their faces. For many years, my lifestyle forced my spouse to serve as both mother and father to our children for periods up to six months at a time. Much of the time away from family was the result of an inability to say "No" to the calls for help from community services. My response to these calls was always "Yes, I'll find the time" — "Yes" to the school board, "yes" to the recreation board, "yes" to the church, and "yes" to hundreds of speaking engagements, all of which took precious time.

Other coaches have even more extreme tales to tell on the subject. One confided to me that he once returned home after a long night in his office watching films to see this note from his wife pinned to the bedspread:

> Paul,
> You haven't given me the time of day. I'm not giving you the time of night.

So it is with many coaching families. The spans of time that go by without any communication are simply too long.

For over 20 years, Dick Vermeil, the retired coach of the Philadelphia Eagles, committed himself completely to the tasks of coaching high school, college, and professional football teams — to the almost total neglect of family. Now he speaks freely of the wrenching problems incurred by his children from having grown up without a father. He also speaks of the anxieties felt by a wife concerned for his emotional health. Only with the guidance of a friend in the clergy and with the recognition by the coach himself that his labors were being lost on men with less driving ambitions, did Vermeil come to recognize what is often called "burn out," a state of physical exhaustion coupled with a perception of ineffectiveness.

Commenting on coaches' "burnout," Davey Johnson, a former professional baseball manager, said, "I still have a burning desire to win but sometimes you get so tired. There has to be a middle ground between living and dying. That is what I am looking for."

Over-commitment of time and burnout are among the most common causes of problems between coaches and their families, but there are others.

To the consternation of some spouses, coaches who are always in the public eye place themselves on a stage and, too often, focus their attentions on the actors who share that stage — athletes, media, boosters, or fans — with spouse and children ever in the background. Equally disturbing to some spouses is the coaches' habit of bringing workday dilemmas to the dinner table or, worse, the bedroom.

At a coaches conference several summers ago I talked with a coaching friend and her husband who had been having progressively worsening problems with their marriage. They relived their past for a few moments, remembering their first meeting in a high school corridor and the occasion of their engagement on a moonlight night beside the Musconetcong River in New Jersey. Even mention of the wedding celebration brought back fond memories of the ceremony, the reception, and a Nordic honeymoon. But, when I asked them about their recent outings together, neither could recall where they had gone or what they had done. They couldn't even remember when they had last gone out together. Their marriage was so centered in the past that they had lost the joy of the present and the hope for the future.

Solutions

Are there any solutions to these dilemmas? I have heard some coaches say that the only answer is to "train" one's spouse to be supportive. Others suggest that marriage and coaching cannot make a happy mix. Neither of these positions presents the best answer. Indeed, a supportive mate who is able to share happily in the trials of the coach's profession and a coach who understands the tensions and burdens of the spouse can form a team of the strongest fibre.

How can such a team be developed? Clearly no one has all the answers. A friend tells the story of a bachelor psychology professor who lectured on "Ten Commandments for Parents." After he got married, he rewrote the lecture and renamed it "Suggestions for Parents." After his second child, he titled it "Hints for Parents." And, after the birth of his third child, he gave up lecturing on the subject altogether!

Still, reflection on my own marriage points to the need to develop experiences in which the entire family can be included. Some of these might even center around job-oriented events. For example, my wife and all my children have shared in basketball scouting excursions. My daughter holds the family reputation for being the most astute opponent-watcher. These trips together have provided time for intimate conversations with family members — conversations that might not otherwise have occurred.

The accompaniment of at least one family member to the annual basketball coaches' convention has provided opportunities for that person to share time with coaching friends, to witness the outstanding games provided by the "Final Four," and to develop an appreciation for some of the pressures common to the coaching profession.

Perhaps of greatest significance to our family development has been the reward of summer togetherness. The epitome of that togetherness occurred in the 1976 final match of a professional tennis tournament in which Jimmy Connors defeated Raul Ramirez. For the match, my children, my wife, and I all served as line umpires.

Because of the school-year demands on coaches — particularly on those involved in speaking appointments, clinic engagements, recruiting, film watching, camp preparations, scouting, and so on — setting aside time during the summer months for fun with family is of paramount importance. We are all familiar with the slogan that "The family that prays together stays together." Equally accurate, I feel, would be the slogan "The family that *plays* together stays together."

Included in my own family's summer rituals has been participation in a variety of conferences of the Fellowship of Christian Athletes. Here my children played with other coaches' children. My wife attended seminars with other coaching wives, itself an enriching and therapeutic encounter for her. And together my wife and I participated with other couples in discussions about problems common to coaching lives. These get-togethers are like a tonic; they are a source of strength with which to face the ordeals of the next year. As alcoholics gain strength from commiseration with others in an Alcoholics Anonymous group, so coaches can build confidence in the knowledge that their life problems are not unlike those faced by many others.

I also suggest that coaches make a conscious and sustained effort to broaden their horizons by developing interests outside their work. Such interests open doors for family conversations not centered on the coach or the coach's work, and they promote rationality by providing a perspective on how relatively unimportant some of a coach's professional work really is.

※ ※ ※ ※ ※

These are difficult times in which to raise children and hold a family together. Strains and stresses pull at us constantly. Our society's emphasis on a higher standard of living places undue economic pressure on those of us who coach and teach. The lure of sex outside marriage is an ever present tug. Both mates today seek more fulfillment through job related experiences. Children suffer from being raised more by television than by parents. They also face the ever-present temptations of drug use so prevalent in many communities. It is an uphill battle to sustain for our families the values and goals we held when starting our families.

But whether coaches are single or married, raising children or taking care of aging parents, they need to recognize that their families are vital to their work and well-being. They must never lose sight of the significance of the family team — a support group without equal. They must nourish that team for the health of all concerned.

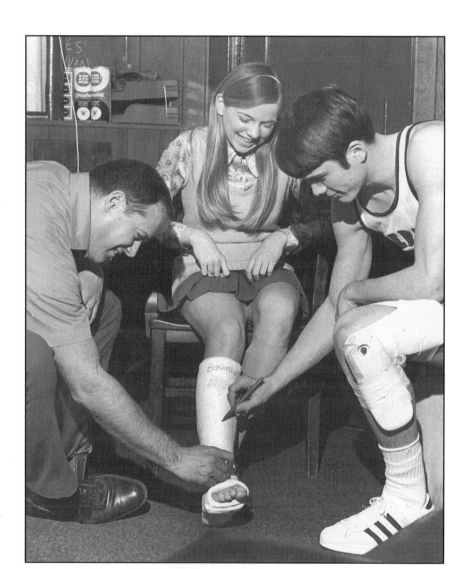

3
FAITH
a guide to philosophical development

Nothing in Life is more wonderful than faith — the one great moving force which we can neither weigh in the balance nor test in the crucible.
Life of Sir William Osler, Harvey Cushing

Undoubtedly the most important choice coaches make is acceptance of a faith to direct their lives. Their faith affects everything about them — their perception of life's meaning, their standards for judging right and wrong, and their goals. Coaches need a philosophy, as was mentioned earlier, and every philosophy is rooted in a faith — an unequivocal belief in something bigger and stronger than the self.

Faith vs Ego

Because sports are so visible, coaches who lead secondary school or collegiate programs often have inflated notions of their own importance. Yearning for the limelight, some even fashion personal trademarks for themselves — the Bryant hat, the Carnesseca sweater, the Thompson "over-the-shoulder" towel, the Lewis checkered towel, the Tarkanian "towel-in-the-mouth," and so on. But personal aggrandizement is a false idol. Indeed, few practices can destroy a coach from within so easily as reliance on image as a coaching tool. Image is simply too shallow. Image doesn't get the job done.

Rather than developing personal images, coaches would be better served developing a solid, substantive faith. Only with faith can they restore traditional values and wholesome goals to their work. Only with faith can they measure successes and failures against coaching goals. Indeed only with faith can coaches have the inner strength to withstand the pressures of their business.

Those who think they can "go it alone" without faith in some form are headed for a fall. Employment as a coach is tenuous; a large percentage of those who begin careers in coaching do not last very long. Many who fall by the wayside can attribute their falls to the feeling of failure, of losing, of frustration, of trying to fly solo before knowing how to fly at all. A rooted faith could have helped them through these moments of dark feelings.

Whenever I hear of a colleague's decision to leave coaching because of feelings of inadequacy, I am reminded of what my family calls "The Saga of Lufthansa." The story has to with the tragedy of Lufthansa Flight 393 ("Zree ninedy zree," my uncle Jack would say in his German accent) which developed engine trouble over the Atlantic Ocean. Captain Wilhelm Von Smidt first announced the failure of the left engine and then the failure of the right. Next he announced that he would "ditch" the plane into the ocean. "Ladies and gentlemen," said the Captain over the intercom, "Please remain calm. Those of you with life vests, please exit the plane through the left exit door. Those of you without life vests — thank you for flying Lufthansa."

If they are to make it in their pressurized work, coaches need faith as a life vest. Without it, they will likely have to "ditch" the profession with the epitaph, "Thank you for your short tenure as a coach."

Faith as Support

I can vividly remember the nights following heart-wrenching losses on the basketball court. On these occasions, thousands of thoughts raced through my mind from evening into the dawn of the next day. Sleepless, I tossed this "mass of madness" through my mind. The game had been like the winds and rains of a tropical typhoon, a stunning fury. The crowd had boiled into anger at times and hurled debris to the floor. The mental replay of every missed opportunity during the game was painful. I experienced agony. I experienced self-doubt and self-pity. I experienced anger. I made excuses. When sleep finally came, it would be interrupted, seemingly within minutes, by someone from the media seeking a quotation over the phone. Awake again, the miserable suffering continued in the recapitulation of the events of the previous evening.

After nights like this, I would rise early, slip quietly from my house, watch the last star fade into the dawn sky, return to the house, and look at my youngsters in peaceful sleep. Only then did some inner urging force me into moments of more rational thought; only then did I find a semblance of tranquility. During these moments, I was reminded that the lost game was, after all, only a lost game — something about which relatively few people cared. I was reminded that I was still alive, that I was in fact a lucky man with a beautiful, supporting family.

Ultimately peace came from the conscious realization that some Greater Being cared and that, whatever the travails of the previous night, the events of that night were meant to be. I can't imagine what twenty-eight years of coaching would have been like had I not found those moments when a peace came from the belief that, in my anxiety, I was not alone and that some good would grow from the despair.

The glitter that often accompanies sporting events and "dogs" the coach's movements makes it very difficult, at times, for the coach to pay attention to bigger matters such as faith. There is great temptation to cast one's faith on the fragile icons of glory, adulation, and fame. To be lauded, then, is the coach who, heaped with acclaim, puts it all aside to focus on matters of substance in his or her work and relationships. A dramatic example of someone who could put fame in perspective was Eric Littel, whose great faith was a feature in the film *Chariots of Fire*. Viewers will recall that Littel, a world class runner, spurned opportunities for glory in sports to pursue a call to work in the ministry. We all enjoy the attention which follows high visibility, but only a few know how to put aside the hoopla, regain perspective, and allow faith to direct our time and our lives to more important needs and deeds.

The idea of regaining perspective brings to mind a story about a ten year old girl on a camping trip. In school, the girl had been hearing a great deal about space ships, UFO's, satellite stations, and Star Wars. One starlit evening she went out with her camp counselor, stared at the heavens for a few moments, and then asked, "Which ones did our scientists shoot up there?"

Of course it is really amazing what modern technology has allowed mankind to do in space exploration. But more amazing yet is the galaxy of stars and the interstellar matter that have made up the heavens for eons — long before NASA. The little girl might have kept this in mind, and coaches who become swept up in their own feelings of importance would do well to put what they do in broader perspective as well — something that can happen when a greater reliance is placed on faith.

There is an irony to the fact that coaches resist the grander perspective and the faith that comes with it. Coaches often insist that their players trust completely in their judgements as coaches. Some rely on the age-worn axiom "Yours is not to question why; yours is just to do or die." And I have heard others say, "Trust in me and I will lead you to glory land" — or words to that effect. At the root of these comments is the insistence by coaches that players trust them. The sad truth, however, is that many coaches refuse to place the same kind of trust in an inner faith that would help them to gain the trust they seek. A few coaches, in fact, renounce faith in any form as a sign of weakness. This is unfortunate, because renunciations of faith shut out the support system coaches need — a system whose importance some do not recognize until calamity touches their lives in lost coaching jobs or family. Only then do some have time for reflection and for seeking help.

Watching the film *The Karate Kid (I)*, I was moved by the message of faith that underscored the relationship between the bullied young lad who had moved to California and his aging Oriental "sensei" who held the secrets of Karate so desired by the boy. Daily, the youngster was put through the onerous tasks of painting and polishing the old man's collection of antique cars with the promise that what he was doing was preparation for Karate. "Trust me," said the sensei. The boy's faith in the old man and his method of teaching Karate technique through practical labors was eventually upheld in victory at a Karate tournament. "Trust me," say coaches. But the desired trust will come only when the coaches, too, can trust.

Inevitably, if one coaches long enough, there comes a feeling that one is not in control. At such times, coaches become struck with the thought that perhaps changes in young people and in the games themselves have passed them by. Often doubt closes in like a cloud, leaving the coach wondering about his professional worth.

For the coach without faith, this can be an agonizing period. Among coaches with faith, however, there is the feeling that they need not be troubled — that a greater strength will always be a companion for counsel and support.

As depicted in the film *Gandhi*, Mahatma Mohandas Gandhi, whose rich life was built on a faith, said, "Whenever I begin to despair, I remember that all through history truth and love have triumphed. Tyranny often seems to rule and be invincible, but at last it is always overthrown. Always."

Definitions of Faith

What is faith? One coaching friend once told me that her faith, her only solace, is sustained in her ability to see good in everything.

Similarly, in his book *Naming the Whirlwind: The Renewal of God-Language*, the prominent theologian Dr. Langdon Gilkey speaks of faith in this way: "The beginning of faith...appears in the awareness of the sacred in the profane, of joy and wonder in the midst of insecurity, of meaning and truth in the midst of meaninglessness, and of life in the face of death."

Albert Einstein, in a Princeton symposium, reportedly also connected faith with "a sense of wonder and awe." According to Einstein, a person "to whom [the] emotion [of peace arising from faith] is a stranger, who can no longer pause to wonder and stand wrapped in awe, is as good as dead: his eyes are closed."

That faith and wonder are connected is further supported by Dr. John Herbert Nichols, former Medical Doctor, Camp Administrator, and Athletic Director at Oberlin College. "All of us can marvel at the accomplishments of great people," Dr. Nichols once told me, "but a person of faith can marvel at the Alaskan Ptarmigan even more." Those familiar with that "fowl of the North" know of its constant change in color to blend with the landscape of the season. "Truly," said Dr. Nichols, "this miracle, impossible to create with man's hand, inspires a real faith."

Coaches of faith are able really to see the unique beauty of the young lives they inspire, to hear an athlete's cry for help, to recognize injustice and inequity, to feel in harmony with those in opposition, to be freed to the truth.

Signs of Faith and its Lack

In a seminar, Robert Buckwalter, a noted New England cleric, has suggested four measures of faith in a person's life: resilience, stamina, inspiration, and initiative.

Resilience is the "incredible capacity of people to bounce back," Buckwalter explains. "Gravely ill, they fight through to recovery. Phased out of a job, they train themselves for another. Uncoupled by divorce, they pull themselves together and begin again."

Stamina, according to Buckwalter, is "the ability to see some worthy enterprise through to the end."

Inspiration is that rare ability to motivate others to action. "Inspirational people," said Buckwalter, "tend to be on the giving end of praise and encouragement much more than they are on the receiving end."

Finally, *initiative* is the characteristic of people who are active in their lives, not merely reactive.

All four — resilience, stamina, inspiration, and initiative — are good measuring sticks for coaches as they reflect on their own faith.

On the other hand, those coaches I have known who lack the strength of faith become so consumed in the development of their own image that they are afraid to have their work critically examined. They tend to lack confidence and to fear that the truth about them will be revealed. They hold to thoughts that are hollow or borrowed. They live their lives with little serenity. They have difficulty in facing each day's crises. What is worst for players, coaches without a base of inner strength often operate at minimum levels of caring and sharing.

※ ※ ※ ※ ※

In the macho world of coaching, discovering a faith to live by can easily be looked upon as a sign of weakness. Yet we all know that America's forefathers chose to engrave the words "In God We Trust" on our coins. These words suggest that the citizens of the United States hold to a faith in God as a measure of strength. Coaches would also be well served to view faith, not as a sign of weakness, but as an indicator of strength. In fact, in the sometimes tempestuous world of coaching athletic teams, a substantive faith — being the coach's only root source of peace — is well worth seeking.

4
RESPONSIBILITY
a coach's charge

Man can will nothing unless he has first understood that he must count on no one but himself, that he is alone, abandoned on earth in the midst of his ultimate responsibilities, without help. With no other aim than the one he sets himself, with no other destiny than the one he forges for himself on this earth.

Le Etre et le néant, Jean Paul Sarte

In the life of a coach, the label of irresponsibility is the ultimate rebuke. I can imagine no facet of human character more subject to ridicule — and possibly even to legal action — than irresponsibility.

Responsibility's Limits

One of the unrecognized dangers in the coaching profession is a lack of understanding as to where a coach's responsibility to his charges begins and where it ends. In the minds of most coaches I know, there is a grey area regarding the subject. Some reflect on their responsibility only in terms of coaching hours or in terms of legality while others include educational and ethical considerations as facets of their responsibility.

As an administrator, I would feel ill at ease with a coach in my charge who defined responsibility purely in terms of time. If coaching comes to be a clock-punch business, much will be lost. Coaching is around-the-clock work. Like good doctors, coaches are always on call.

I would also feel ill at ease with a coach in my charge who defined responsibility in purely legal terms. A coach's responsibilities are moral as well as legal.

David Held of Claremont, California, told of a widowed Hispanic mother who died in a rural area of Southern California leaving a family of eight children. The oldest, a seventeen year old daughter, took upon herself the burden of caring for the family. "The neighbors watched her as she took up the task with courage, keeping the children clean, well-fed, and in school," relates Held. A year later a friend complimented her on her achievements. The young girl pushed aside credit, saying only, "It was something I *had* to do."

It is this sense of moral obligation that separates the better coaches from the clock-punch crowd. Good coaches carry out their responsibilities simply because they *have to*. Recognition that one has the responsibility of leading, it seems to me, is essential to a fruitful coaching experience. Through caring about players' attitudes and actions and through example in their own lives, coaches can always establish a responsible pattern to their ways.

Tales of Irresponsibility

I recall in vivid detail two happenings in which more than considerable embarrassment accompanied failures to act responsibly. One of these involved me and the other, a close friend.

When I was an undergraduate, the elderly landlady of the private residence in which a roommate and I lived died suddenly. The following morning, shortly after my roommate had left for a class, I was informed by a nurse that Mrs. Johnson was dead. I felt deeply saddened because Mrs. Johnson and I had become quite close friends; she often requested my presence in the evenings to read the newspaper to her in her spacious living room.

With the news of the death, my roommate immediately moved out. I was asked by Mrs. Johnson's daughter to stay on, rent free, for the duration of the school year to keep the house occupied, control the temperature, mow the lawn, feed the cat, *etc.* I willingly accepted the responsibility placed on me.

On the day after Mrs. Johnson's death, her casket, now bedecked with floral arrangements, was returned to the huge living room for viewing. She lay there in peaceful repose in the open casket for two days, adorned in a beautiful silk taffeta dress. Mourners and well-wishers dropped by to pay their respects to the family. In the evening, with the lights dimmed, the family would retreat to a nearby motel leaving me alone with the deceased as resident caretaker for the night hours.

Sometime during the early morning hours of the day of the funeral, the cat somehow escaped from my bedroom and, in its own manner of expressing sorrow, climbed atop the corpse and soiled Mrs. Johnson's dress. To my chagrin and utter consternation, my efforts to remove the smudge marks from her dress were to no avail. In my frenzy, I finally called the mortuary and explained my plight. A hurried house call by "Digger" Moreland, as he was affectionately called, armed with some cleaning solutions and an artfully arranged floral bouquet saved the day only moments before the bereaved family gathered at the house for one last viewing. Until now, the secret of that memorable morning has lain hidden with Digger and me. But my embarrassment for the irresponsible oversight of allowing the cat to soil the dress has haunted me for years.

The second happening involved one of the kindest, most gentle humans I have known — a fellow counselor at a boys camp in Maine. Twice he had been selected for the Knight's Award, which was presented to the counselor who best represented chivalry and other knightly virtues. He was so adored by campers that each summer many requested placement in his cabin.

Each cabin took one weekend excursion each summer. These were always joyous events, planned and arranged jointly by counselors and campers. Some groups chose hiking excursions in the nearby mountains; others, canoe trips on the lakes and rivers of the region. My friend and his crew decided to traverse Big Sebago Lake by canoe and to camp on Frye's Island, known for its sandy beaches. The trip went smoothly until nightfall. In the course of outlining "the plan for the morrow," a nightly ritual on trips, the counselor neglected to review the checklist of *do*'s and *don't*'s — the camp rules governing the conduct of campers while on trips.

At dawn, the exhilarated and excited campers were up and running on the beach. As the counselor slept, a couple of the lads who had drifted far from the campsite decided to cool off in the fresh waters. In a freak accident, unexplained even today, one of the boys crashed his head against a rock, lost consciousness, and drowned. In panic, his comrade ran back to the campsite for help. A short time later, the boy's lifeless body was pulled from lake water only two feet deep.

No amount of counsel or sympathetic consoling could revive the anguish which had befallen the stricken counselor. His confessed irresponsibility will torment his life forever.

Not all such acts have such dramatic and irrevocable conclusions. But experiences like these can serve as reminders to coaches, who are often placed in circumstances of responsibility for young lives and their actions. Our antennae must constantly be extended in anticipation of judgements we will be called upon to make.

My experience with acts of irresponsibility is that they are no more often committed by unscrupulous people than by well-meaning people who do not realize that they are acting irresponsibly.

Responsible Decisions

The moments when coaches become most prone to irresponsible behavior occur when they are emotionally involved in the conduct of a game. These are moments when reason tends to escape us, and the goal of seeking victory looms as a dragon before our eyes. They are moments in coaches' lives when they are most vulnerable to the temptations of what, in more reflective moments, might be recognized as irresponsible.

For that reason, I applaud the actions taken by a coach during an intercollegiate basketball game in Northern Ohio, a bastion of basketball battles. It had been the final day of exams for the home college, and the students, many inebriated, were revelling in the pre-Christmas excitement and in the rare treat of playing a good team for the conference championship. An air of volatility filled the gymnasium. With about five minutes left on the clock in the first half, the visiting team possessed a small lead.

Then a player from the visiting team, in an attempt to block a shot, unceremoniously fouled a home player on a breakaway. Both players toppled to the floor, and the visiting player was rightly charged with a foul. But, while graciously aiding the fouled player to his feet, the player who committed the foul was rushed and pummelled by a handful of intoxicated "student security" men who poured from the bleachers—people whose role was to maintain decorum at the game. Officials, coaches, and players worked at restoring order in what was, by then, a very charged atmosphere.

Before play was resumed, the visiting Athletic Director and assistant coaches requested of the local Athletic Director that town police be alerted to potential violence in the gym and asked to have officers posted. The suggestion was rejected by the home Director on the grounds that police were "unnecessary," and the game continued.

Moments later, the tall and talented center of the visiting team reached towards the bleachers for an errant pass and was raked by a spectator with a crisp right to the face. The blow smashed the center's nose and broke his spectacles. The player fell in a bloody heap on the floor. Then the stands emptied, and an angry and crazed crowd rained blows on players from the visiting team. Desperately, the coaches and captains tried to prevail on the scores of students to release their guests and allow them to escape to their locker room.

The visiting coach had another brief conversation with the home team's embarrassed Athletic Director, who could do no more than "hope" for improved crowd behavior. Then the visiting coach ordered his team to shower, dress, and prepare for departure. Amidst a hail of epithets, the bus left the parking lot.

Most coaches take certain things as given. They know that, once a game is started, they should see it to fruition; they avoid the labels that accompany their forfeiting a game; they avoid actions that might bring the criticism of peers on them for deviations from accepted practices. The action of the visiting coach therefore ran counter to his coaching instincts. But my sense is that his decisions were the responsible ones.

Growing as a coach is sometimes a difficult struggle. It involves pain. It involves risk. It even involves letting go of things with which coaches are comfortable and moving into the unknown. The demonic in us sometimes lures us into believing that it is only human to do something that grabs attention, puts us in the limelight, or is risqué. In our eagerness to "do our things" we occasionally forget that our larger responsibility is to those with whom we work. Coaches should anticipate these peoples' needs and fill them to the best of their ability, concerned with the good of those in their charge.

I therefore applaud the responsible actions of a high school football coach whose champion team was one of the strongest in the South. The team was scheduled to play an extremely weak opponent whose numbers of athletes were reduced by a measles epidemic, a team they had beaten the year before by a score of 78-0. The champion coach called and offered to cancel the game, and the offer was accepted. Although there was much to be gained in terms of regional ranking from another lopsided victory, the game should have been canceled because of the physical harm that was almost certain to befall the weaker team. The offer to cancel the game was not only an act of charity but an extremely responsible act as well.

※ ※ ※ ※ ※

No one ever said that coaching would be easy, or safe, or simple. Nothing worthwhile is. But the good news is that, responsibly lived, a coach's life can be one of the most rewarding and fulfilling imaginable.

5
LIKEABLE IMAGE
a coaching asset

> Because I am idolatrous and have besought,
> With grievous supplication and consuming prayer,
> The admirable image that my dreams have wrought.
> *Epigram*, Ernest Dewson

Like many whose professions involve close relationships with others, coaches get their greatest satisfaction from the recognition, respect, admiration, and affection they receive from those they touch in their work. Nothing — with the possible exception of an exhilarating victory resulting from sound preparation and execution — moves coaches as much as the feeling that people admire them and their efforts.

Then why aren't all coaches admired? In explaining why praise and admiration seem to fall naturally on some coaches and eludes others, one coach has made the oversimplified suggestion to me that the level of esteem bestowed on a coach is dictated solely by the coach's personality. There may be some truth to this. But, having reviewed many situations in which coaches have been denied the praise and admiration they want, I have come to believe that the villain is not so much failings in personality as the public projection of an image that does not serve the coach well. Sometimes, through lack of attention or sensitivity, coaches transmit the wrong messages to players, fans, representatives of the media, parents, and others. Thus unfortunate images of the coaches take form — images with which coaches must make their peace. Far better that coaches consciously nurture an image useful to their purposes and true to their selves than to be victimized in their work by inaccurate images composed by others.

Pat Riley, the former Los Angeles Laker coach, has expressed that coaches should be judged on "image, and control, and organization." Sam McManis, in a *Los Angeles Times* article about Riley, quotes the Laker coach further. Said Riley, "Image and control are probably the two most important.... The image is not how well I dress and my hair. It is how people perceive you. If its [an image] of control and strength, then that's a positive."

Vanity

One factor contributing to poor image is vanity. Coaches' excessive pride in their own appearance, qualities, or achievements is easily revealed to public scrutiny, and it can easily translate into disaffection. Coaches who strut the sidelines or courtsides bedecked like peacocks in full plumage and projecting an air of importance certainly attract attention — but rarely affection.

A sign of excessive pride is the post-victory interview punctuated with the word "I" — a word which, when overused, quickly alienates the affections of listeners. Here, for example, is a quotation from a tape recording made by a student newspaper reporter during a post-game interview with a midwestern college football coach:

> I never thought I'd pull it out. The guys did just what I asked of them. The [winning play] was one I had put together over the objections of a couple of my assistants and put in only this week. It was a pretty nice one if I do say so myself. When I sent it in, I knew that, if the kids didn't botch it up, it would win me the game.

Even if all this was true, it would have been better left unsaid. To gain the affection of the public, this coach should have been more humble.

Terms like "modest" certainly do not describe Howard Cosell, a sports commentator renowned for his vanity. Cosell's 'tell-it-like-it-is' approach to life seems at times only an obnoxious way for him to toot his own horn. In his book *I Never Played the Game*, Cosell lives up to his reputation of vanity and boastfulness. "Who the hell made *Monday Night Football* unlike any other sports program on the air," he asks. "If you want the plain truth, I did."

When I read this verbiage, I am reminded of the man, enamored with his own greatness, who asked his wife, "Honey, how many great men do you think there are in this world?" Her quick response was, "I'm not sure, darling, but there is one less than you think."

Even those who admire striking appearance and positive accomplishments seem to admire them most in those who accept their gifts and successes without exaggerated bravura. <u>Accomplishment accompanied by a humble, meek, or gentle countenance seems far more palatable.</u>

Sports buffs who watched the 1983 World Series between the Philadelphia Phillies and the Baltimore Orioles on television were likely as moved as I was by the humble candor of one member of the ABC coverage team, Earl Weaver. Partly because the immodest Howard Cosell was also in the booth, Weaver's tone was refreshing. On a number of occasions when he could have beat his chest over his own achievements as former manager of the Orioles, Weaver instead praised the efforts of his managerial successor, Joe Altobelli, and the players who performed so admirably under Altobelli's tutelage. Weaver's kind words not only raised appreciation for Altobelli, but also reflected favorably on the gracious donor.

Some Humble People

For many summers I have worked at the Volvo International Tennis Tournament in North Conway, New Hampshire—now situated in New Haven, Conneticut. The tournament has been one of the popular stops for the touring men professionals. There, in my role as a tournament administrator, I observe at close range fan reaction to the various players. Inevitably, even little-known players develop a close and adoring following when they accept public attention and accolades humbly. Conversely, those who are unresponsive, pompous, or self-adoring are met with much less affection.

Calvin Smith, one of America's foremost track hopefuls for the 1984 Olympics, displayed an unaffected style following his 200 meter win at the 1983 World Championships in Helsinki. Asked if it bothered him that the media was more interested in the exploits of the great Carl Lewis than in his own marvelous victory, Smith said simply, "The Lord gets the credit for all of us anyway." <u>Such modesty is a welcome relief</u>, and it sets well with a public that wants to adore its sports heroes.

Tracy Caulkins, the elegant swimmer whose accomplishments in the 1984 Olympics captured the imaginations of viewers throughout the world, was asked following her last gold-medal win how it felt to have stood above all. Tracy's calm reply was that she was gratified in the wins mostly for the happiness it brought to her family, her coaches, and her country. How refreshing an image of one so <u>caring about those around her</u>!

And Bill Bradley, the "super shot" of collegiate basketball in the 1960's, an outstanding member of the New York Knicks and later a United States Senator from New Jersey, was another athlete whose quiet lack of pretentiousness lent to his favorable public image. Following the 1965 NCAA basketball tournament in which the Princeton senior broke the scoring record for one tournament game, he was asked to describe his greatest thrill as a collegiate athlete. One would have guessed that his answer would have included some mention, at least, of Bradley's marvelous scoring feat. But Bradley answered, "My greatest thrill in basketball has been the opportunity to play with these 11 guys who are my teammates."

More Humble People

I recall being called upon in a college English Literature class to write a paper describing the personalities who had most influenced my life. One of those about whom I chose to write was a former college professor of public speaking, Dr. John F. Smith, who had been obliged to retire at the young age (for him at least) of 70. For years, Smith was one of the more popular figures in the college community. His classes, it seems, bulged with early registrations—despite the fact that he also held a reputation for being a strict grader. His love of teaching and of young people was always reflected in a gentle rapport with students. For decades, Smith's home, which was across the street from the gymnasium, served as a refuge from dormitory life for scores of students, who found Professor Smith and his wife loving and caring surrogate parents, counselors, and friends.

Following Smith's retirement from classroom teaching, he persuaded the college's administration to permit his continued affiliation with the college as the custodian of the gymnasium! In this capacity, he was able to retain close contacts with students.

When I was appointed basketball coach at the college, I became reacquainted with Dr. Smith. The newer generations of students, of course, knew Smith only as a custodian, but they had no less affection for him than their predecessors.

Seeing Smith in the role of janitor, I developed an even deeper admiration for this modest man, so unaffected by titles and status, who led his life by the dictates of decency. I recall with gratitude the lessons of life shared by "Prof" Smith even as he neared his second retirement, almost 20 years after the first! Without fail, the morning following each basketball game, a short, hand-written note in his aging scrawl would appear on my freshly-dusted desk with a message, sometimes quoted, but always appropriate to the lessons surrounding the happenings of the previous night's game. I kept some of those notes for many years. Most were lost in the passage of time but each, regardless of the game's outcome, accented the virtues of humility which were so much a part of this beautiful man.

"Give even a thimbleful of love," Smith once wrote, "and you'll receive an ocean full of joy." It is true. For me, knowing Smith was an introduction to humble living and has served as a periodic reminder of my need to foster a better image by keeping my head at a level where I can "eyeball" the poor as well as the rich, the dumb as well as the smart, the janitors as well as the presidents. People like Smith differ from many others because they seem to withstand the corroding effects of daily life. Fatigue, despair, and depression rarely chip away at their constant goodness. They seem masters of their environments as most of us are not. A finely-tuned humility is the common denominator among them.

The person of this century most commonly acknowledged for his goodness and as truly humble in a non-violent way was Mahatma Mohandas Gandhi. A touch of his grand capacity to use meekness as a tool for the strengthening growth of his adoring followers was depicted in the well-known film of his life called *Gandhi*. In one memorable sequence of the film, a frenzied Hindu man, coming to a bedridden Gandhi weakened by long fasting, says, "I am going to hell anyway, but I do not want to go with death on my soul." Gandhi asks why he is suggesting such a thing. With his eyes reflecting a deep anguish, the Hindu man extends his hand waist high, and answers: "I killed a Muslim child. I bashed his head against a wall. [The Muslims] killed my son and he was only about so high." Gandhi pauses and then whispers, "I know a way out of hell." Extending his own hand beside the bed, he continues, "Find a little boy about so high whose parents have both been killed, and raise him as your own son." Straining to be heard, Gandhi adds: "Just be sure he is a Muslim boy, and that you raise him as a Muslim." With torment suddenly leaving his eyes, the man drops to his knees beside Gandhi's bed in tears. Gandhi, in turn, reaches out to touch him.

In coaching, there have also been those whose strength of leadership lay, not in vanity or persuasive rhetoric, but in the humility of their actions — men and women of stature whose humble influence imparts meaning to the lives of many young people. John Nichols, Gertrude Moulton, and John Wooden come immediately to mind as people of that mold. Their fine deeds, like those of Smith and Gandhi, are most realized when their positive influence moves others to make better of their own lives. In no profession is the opportunity for such influence greater than in our own.

Commitment

A characteristic found in coaches with favorable images is the ability to make honorable commitments. So vital is commitment, in fact, that some long-time coaches view it as the first step to achievement on athletic fields and courts. Truly there are rewards aplenty for those whose lives are committed to effort with excellence as a goal.

Many good things happen around the lives of coaches who possess a high degree of commitment to their work. The most recognized trait that I have seen in committed persons is a very noticeable self-confidence. People who have committed themselves seem to feel better about themselves and, consequently, to have a heightened trust of others. This, in turn, improves relationships with others and raises the others' own self-esteem. And, when players or parents or peers are made to feel good about themselves, the image they have of the coach who made them feel that way is one that commands respect.

Attitude

A coach's attitude also determines whether the coach's image is likeable. All too frequently, coaches think of bad attitude as a problem of athletes, not coaches. But attitude is a two-way street: good coaches have discovered that their own attitudes toward others determine others attitudes toward them. Normally, good coaching attitudes will foster good athletic responses and results.

If coaches project an image that reflects negativism — an attitude in which the word 'can't' is emphasized or an attitude of defeat — little can be expected in the form of positive responses from athletes.

Don Swartz, once an internationally recognized swimming coach and now a respected lecturer on creative performance in sport, has said,

> Wherever you find a person doing an outstanding job and getting outstanding results, you'll find a person with a good attitude. Such people seem to have one thing in common — they expect more good out of life than bad; they expect to succeed more often than they fail — and they do.

For coaches to realize life at this level, they must first have the self-image they want to have.

Few coaches I have known have felt so good about themselves that they have freed themselves from the bindings that moor them as hostages to their jobs. There is, however, a growing band of happy, very productive coaches

LIKEABLE IMAGE 31

whose attitudes are so positive that potential problems rarely reach fruition for them.

"Treat every person as the most important person on earth," advises Swartz. "There is nothing in the world that men, women and children want and need more than self-esteem, the feeling that they're important, that they're needed, that they're respected." Recipients of this attention will give in return their love, respect, and support to the coach who fills this need. Both parties, then, will benefit from the good attitude that coaches can nurture.

* * * * *

It is well for coaches to be concerned with what others see in them. When their colleagues and those who see them work respect them and their efforts, it is easier for coaches to establish good relationships with others and to do their jobs effectively.

6
DEVELOPING CONFIDENCE
a test of positive thinking

> The mutual confidence on which all else depends can be maintained only by an open mind and a brave reliance upon free discussion.
>
> Learned Hand

It was the occasion of the Final Four NCAA basketball tournament and, as was our custom, my wife and I had gone out for dinner to a Southern-style restaurant with a cluster of coaching friends and their spouses. A number of coaches in the group had endured particularly difficult seasons that year, and they complained about their teams loudly. Each, in turn, attributed their "downer" seasons to player inadequacies — poor abilities or low levels of self-confidence.

After dinner, my wife, exasperated by the negative tones of the conversations she had endured, said, "Show me a coach who can be *positive* and you will have shown me a real coach."

I was startled by her out-of-character pronouncement, and I asked her what had triggered it. Ever the sponge in social settings involving groups of coaches, soaking up what is going on around her but offering little in small talk, my wife offered this insightful explanation: "It seems to me that too many coaches I hear blame poor seasons on poor material. I think it's a cop-out." She may be right.

Coincidentally, during the Oldtimer's Round Table at that same convention, a retired coach compared modern collegiate coaches to those of yesteryear. "Today's coach," he intoned, "goes out and hustles talent to put on the floor. In my day we had to prepare for the fray with whatever walked through our doors." Perhaps, as some modern coaches are discovering in reading the old basketball manuals by Clair Bee and others, there is something to be learned from listening to the former mentors.

Out of necessity, these coaches spent far more hours than modern coaches honing skill and instilling confidence in their players through a variety of time consuming methods. Even today, in sports where it is difficult to recruit players who are already polished and confident, coaches prepare for their seasons with greater emphasis on skill development — development that will lead to heightened levels of confidence and so to upgraded athletic performances.

It may be well that we all take notice of such practices. If Ralph Waldo Emerson was correct in his statement that "confidence is having done a thing before," perhaps there is good reason for coaches to plan so that, in the preparation process, athletes will — whether in practice sessions or in the off season — do the things that will make their confidence grow.

Preparation

Solid preparation is the first step towards eliminating players' doubts. Real confidence is a state that reflects little or no doubt or uncertainty. If coaches can instill in athletes' minds the belief that they can prepare for absolutely any eventuality, coaches will have gone a long way toward building confidence.

Many who follow college football can remember the events leading up to the 1984 Orange Bowl contest between Nebraska and Miami. Nebraska had been touted by many in the American press as the strongest football team of the century — better even than the great Army teams of Glenn Davis and Doc Blanchard and the Four Horsemen squads at Notre Dame. But the articles saying that Nebraska couldn't lose did not in fact stop them from losing. Howard Schnellenberger, the Miami coach, had done a grand job of preparing his team. For weeks leading up to the game, he began shaping beliefs — not only those of his players, but those of the entire Miami community. He did a masterful job of telling all who would listen exactly how Nebraska could be beaten. He put aside all doubts that may have haunted his team about their ability to defeat the Nebraska squad, and, curiously, those doubts crept over to haunt the Nebraska contingent. It was the Miami team, which had prepared for any eventuality, that played the game with full confidence. Miami players did not think "We are playing Nebraska!" — a thought that surely would have instilled some doubt. Instead, they thought of themselves as playing a team whose every formation and every move was anticipated.

I recall another occurrence that illustrates how preparation can eliminate self-defeating, confidence-shattering doubt. On the day prior to Harold Solomon's playing Jimmy Connors in the final of the Volvo Tennis Tournament in New Hampshire, Solomon was asked in a news conference about his perceptions of the upcoming match. It was evident to those of us observing that Solomon had real doubts about his chances in the final, but, because he couldn't admit those doubts to the press, he began to explain what he would have to do to beat Connors. The more he developed his explanation, the more confidence he seemed to gain. A plan began to unfold in his mind. At the press conference following the final match, Solomon admitted that only at the previous day's press meeting did a plan of attack for the Connors match come into focus for him. Concentration on that plan and not on a seemingly invincible opponent had made it possible for Solomon to win. The preparation here was mental, but it was preparation nevertheless.

Confidence and Familiarity

Something that coaches should strive to do in confidence building is to develop for their players a familiarity with the situations in which they will be competing. To a certain extent, this can be accomplished with films, but athletes are better served when they have a sense of the nuances of a particular game site and its environment.

Most of us are familiar with the sojourns of world class skiers to venues halfway around the world in search of knowledge about the peculiarities of slopes where major downhill or slalom races will be run. Sometimes the only picture available may be a word-picture, but the effect is the same.

An understanding of what conditions will be like for a competition helps to build a sense of confidence in the performers' abilities to execute their skills in that milieu. A rehearsal or practice in the setting builds confidence even more.

Small Improvements

In sports like swimming or track and field, top performances can often be realized by breaking down expected improvement levels into smaller segments. For example, an intense focus on improving times for the third leg of a 100 meter backstroke event may be necessary to conquer the mental blocks that had slowed a swimmer's performance in that stage of each race.

Often, an ultimate goal can be broken down into lower, more reachable standards, which are progressively raised. Regardless of the talent level with which coaches are working, relative goals can be set and reached.

Track coaches working with potentially record-breaking athletes often try to develop the belief in the athlete that the current record in the event of interest is attainable. Certainly, if athletes are led to believe that the record is insurmountable, they won't break the record, and motivation for improvement will be dampened.

Praise

Keith Bell, a sports psychologist, has warned coaches not to praise athletes so much that they become satisfied with their performances. According to Bell, indiscriminate praise is injurious because it dilutes its intent, which is presumably to bolster confidence and self-image.

Bull Curry, head football coach at the University of Kentucky, is adamant in denunciation of praise. He has said of it in the *NCAA News*,

> I teach that praise is more dangerous than criticism, and both are extremely dangerous. Both can destroy what you are trying to achieve....The instant you begin to believe you are Mr. Wonderful, you get your teeth knocked out. It happens every time.

In the early stages of skill learning, praise may be called upon to overcome discouragement or failure. But, even then, caution should be taken to avoid praise in effusive form. There is a danger that a student might interpret an unrestrained expression of praise as an indication that the coach is satisfied with the level of performance — or, worse, as an indication the coach thinks the athlete has "arrived." Praise must not be overused.

Yet praise can be a useful tool in coaching. In addition to being a cure for discouragement, it can be an instrument for providing instructional information. For example, using an expression like "You are hitting your forehand marvelously" can be as useful in instructing a player as showing the player how to hit the squash forehand.

Phil Simms, the New York Giant quarterback, credits praise from his college coach with building confidence in his own career. He recalls his coach comparing Simms' skills to those of another player who had been tutored by that coach and later became a pro. "You've got everything he's got, and more," Simms remembers his coach saying. "That made me work harder,"

Simms continued, "because [the coach] convinced me I had the talent to make the work worthwhile."

Caution should be the byword in passing out praise, however. While praise can be used to instruct and motivate, praise for performances that are less than good is more apt to lessen confidence levels than to raise them.

Affirmation

Affirmation has become a popular coaching ploy for improving individual performances. Athletes are encouraged to be expressive in a "positive" way — to say things like "I am a winner," "I can accomplish my goals," or "I will do it." The intent is to develop a feeling that stays with the athlete.

Problems arise, however, when athletes who have made positive affirmations lose or fail in an undertaking. Then doubt creeps in and confidence is lost. The athletes may develop the nagging feeling that they are going to fail regardless of what they do. Affirmative statements, to be useful, must be realistic; they must reflect goals that are attainable.

The Positive Use of Doubt

Doubt, obviously, is the primary killer of confidence. And doubt can almost never be entirely eliminated from the minds of young athletes. When it has seemingly been swept under the rug forever, it raises its ugly head again in the strangest of forms and at the most inopportune occasions.

Yet coaches should not despair. Instead, they should attempt to plant the seed of doubt where and when it will work in a positive way for the athlete.

How, one might ask, can the creation of doubt work positively? One answer is that athletes can learn to doubt their own inability. A New England gymnastics coach used this principle well in working with athletes on the balance beam. This coach encouraged the athletes to doubt that they were able to lose balance on their dismounts — a backhanded approach to making positive use of a negative factor. Such an approach allows athletes to live with some uncertainty without crushing their confidence in their ability to perform.

De-emphasizing Winning

Another effective way of building confidence that is rarely considered is to diffuse the importance of winning. My experience has shown that, when winning becomes the focal point of our instructional experience as coaches, we place excessive pressure on players — sometimes to the point where anything less than a winning performance drains confidence out of the athlete. At the least, a focus on winning draws attention away from the execution of those techniques that would make winning possible.

Jimmy Arias, the former "Boy Wonder" of professional tennis, has suffered in recent years from the pressure of being labeled America's next male tennis superstar and from having lost to Stefan Edberg of Sweden in the semifinals of the 1984 Olympic tennis exhibition. Said Arias,

> Everyone in America is so big on winning, winning. The pressure is ridiculous, especially for younger players. It is different for guys like the Swedes...[T]hey have a good attitude. They have fun.

Arias is suggesting that much of his loss of confidence in recent years has been created by the expectations placed on him to win.

* * * * *

Confidence building, which must not be confused with psychoanalysis or other mind games, can be a useful tool in coaching. It is more akin to the systematic stacking of blocks by a child. It begins with sound preparation, and it follows the strategies of acquainting athletes with performance environments and of breaking goals down into measurable segments. Lastly, it calls on coaches to use positive approaches as ways to build confidence in athletes.

7
INNOVATION
a remedy for boredom

> An important scientific innovation rarely makes its way by gradually winning over and converting its opponents; it rarely happens that Saul becomes Paul. What does happen is that its opponents gradually die out and that the growing generation is familiarized with the idea from the beginning.
>
> *The Philosophy of Physics*, Max Planck

Modern coaches cannot constantly change the format of their coaching schemes. That would be too unsettling for even the most mature of athletes. But the occasional introduction of new ideas is a sound coaching practice that brings a sense of optimism to athletic teams and a freshness to athletic performances. More importantly, it helps to relieve tedium and restore concentration to the task of constant preparation.

M-n-M

Almost all the basketball seasons I can remember have reached a period that has called for some novelty or innovation, especially in the construction of the practice sessions. When my coaching staff and I sensed a staleness setting into practice sessions, we would jokingly say to one another, "It's time for an M-n-M."

Here "M-n-M" means, not the sugar-coated candy, but Manuel Nuñoz Martinez. When I knew Manuel, he was a ten-year-old who could shinny up a coconut palm with a bolo in his teeth as fast as any kid on Silliman Beach on the Philippine Island of Negros. He lived across from the hacienda where I resided during my short teaching tenure at Silliman University, and he took me in as a kind of big brother. In fact, he became my constant companion, accompanying me on long treks into the nearby leech-infested jungles and into the mountain caves.

M-n-M also guided me on shell forays along the mollusk-strewn beaches and sand bars that jutted like long fingers into the coral-carpeted Philippine Sea. We often set out together from these sandbars like snorkel-bedecked gladiators, searching the clear waters for the sea shells so famous to the region.

Invariably, the collections of shell specimens we stuffed into the small canvas bags attached to our waists hid creatures of the deep called hermit crabs. The crabs themselves were rarely visible because they burrowed deep into their curled shells at the slightest vibration.

To remove these crabs from their shells, other shell hunters would lay their finds on tinfoil and put them out to "sun" for a week or so — a process that dried out the hermit so that its parched remains could easily be shaken out of its shell. The problem with the process, discovered M-n-M, was that the sun also stole some of the luster from the shells' surfaces, diminishing their worth. But the shells in M-n-M's collection maintained an uncommon glossy radiance. The secret, he showed me, lay in the process of crab removal. Each evening following our sojourns to the sea, he buried our treasures in moistened sand adjacent to a red ant hill. By morning, without fail, each shell would be clean, odorless, bright, and ready for display, the crab removal accomplished by the work of the ants.

To say that my friend M-n-M was an innovative lad would be an understatement. How often I have wished for a similar creativity in the construction of my own daily tennis or basketball practice sessions!

Boredom

Sports seasons hold the potential for being fun-filled learning experiences that athletes can remember with joy. But they also have the potential for being boring. When they are, it's often because practice sessions have become repetitive and predictable. Monotony can take its toll very easily.

My experience as a college football player epitomized the boredom of which I speak. From the first day of practice in September until the last in November, each day varied little from the previous one. On the field at 4:00 pm...twenty minutes of grass drill...twenty minutes on the sled...hup, hup, hike — right shoulder...hup, hup, hike — left shoulder...one hour of play review...huddle...call the play...charge ahead five steps and repeat...ten minutes of wind sprints. Ho hum! We longed for Tuesdays when the monotonous routine would be broken by a twenty minute "live" scrimmage. (Fortunately Bob Agler, the coach my senior year, restored my love for football with variation in the practice sessions and the most imaginative scheme of plays and defenses I have ever seen.)

It is advisable for coaches — young ones, especially — to chart their seasons in an effort to find a pattern to team performance. If a trend of less than zealous performance appears toward the middle or latter part of the season, it may well be attributed to student boredom.

Change of drills or of the timing of drills in a practice session may help. Introducing elements of competition or cancelling a practice altogether are other means by which coaches can grab players' attention and reduce staleness. Most importantly, coaches should make every effort to create an environment that welcomes a change of pace.

Realizing considerable frustration at the rapidity with which tedium was taking hold of tennis practices in my early years coaching the women at Williams College, I solicited the counsel of Clarence Chaffee, former men's coach there and a national champion in the senior division. He introduced me to a series of innovative, spirited drills that infused conditioning techniques, competition, and technical development into the practice regimen. Working these drills into practices recharged my own enthusiasm and that of the students as well.

Taking Risks

Change may come in the form of something dramatic or "risky." Risk-taking is a form of innovation that all coaches need to carry in their briefcases for special moments.

Success has a way of developing in most coaches a conservative frame of mind, a tendency not to stray very far from the zones in which they feel safe. But occasions sometimes dictate the need to try something "bold" — either to break a lethargy and spice up a game, or merely to create some excitement within the players.

In addition, coaches may well be advised to take some risks for their own good. Success tends to breed fear of failure, and fear of failure can be an added weight in our efforts to achieve the ultimate. It is healthy occasionally to "throw caution to the wind" and go for it. Providing an environment that allows risk-taking can, in itself, be a creative form of innovation in coaching.

I have also discovered in preparing teams for risk-filled game plans — especially for contests they were expected to lose — that motivation was fueled by hope and that concentration became focused on the exciting plan. Even in defeat, if whetted by excitement and imagination, the competition was made more enjoyable.

Examples of Innovation

November is a torturous month of preparation for basketball seasons. The most exciting November that one of my teams has ever experienced was one in which I discovered a way to have the players "enjoy" the torture. Moving away from the traditional plan of opening practices with stretching exercises under my direction, I arranged for a talented, statuesque, female student who taught aerobic dance to take over. Clad in leotards, she led the group with musical accompaniment in a stretching routine of aerobics that made them more fit and invigorated than I would have imagined possible. I credit the innovative routines of "Coach" Traylor for a season in which our team did not suffer a single serious injury.

I was intrigued once by an article I had read in a coaching journal about a basketball offensive plan that seemed different from most I had seen. I wrote to the author for more details, and he wrote back saying, "You haven't seen anything yet." He then forwarded to me the description of a new offense that he called "The Layup Only Attack." I found it interesting, but what was even more interesting was a conversation I had with the author several years later, when I asked him about the "Layup Only Attack." "You know," he said, "I devised that because, the year before, we had a shot selection problem on our team. The 'Layup Only' plan didn't really work, but it did make my team much more conscious of selection. We were a better team for having introduced it."

A tennis coaching friend, following a year in which his team had suffered from such internal friction that his players actually rooted against each other, devised a scheme that he credits with restoring positive team feelings. He determined that each player would have a nickname and that each would use the nicknames in conversations with teammates. The plan seemed to break the tension, and collegiality improved immediately.

Basketball fans delight in the innovative dimensions that particular players bring to the game. Any "hooked" follower of the sport has thrilled in the "skyhook" which was introduced to the game by Kareem Abdul Jabbar, the "walking in air" slam dunk of Julius Erving, and the "no look" passes of Larry Bird and Earvin Johnson. Little fanfare accompanied The Sikma Move, however, despite its innovative design — probably because it lacked the ballet-like grace of the other movements. It's peculiar, jerky motion, though, has extended the playing career of its orginator, Jack Sikma. Curtis Bunn of *Newsday* has described the Sikma Move as follows: "It calls for a 180 degree pivot, a step back, and a shot from way behind the head. If someone tries to block it, the pivot foot is still in place, so Sikma can fake the shot and go past the defender." With the help of his college coach, Sikma invented the unique move to compensate for a lack of comparative speed to those other big men he played against.

The above mentioned accounts are but a few examples of innovative designs brought to sport. The most important aspect of each of these is that they represent the introduction of fresh designs to the routine of competition or practice for competition and, often, will be the catalysts to greater joy for participants in competitive experiences.

※ ※ ※ ※ ※

Innovative coaching—sometimes no more than the employment of a change of pace from the ordinary routine — will add vitality to the students under a leader's tutelage. And innovation in the planning of practice sessions and game plans may be the spice that lends joy and satisfaction to the coaching experience as well.

8
LISTENING
an art for the tough and tender

> Upon a mountain height, far from the sea,
> I found a shell,
> And to my listening ear the lonely thing
> Ever a song of ocean seemed to sing,
> Ever a tale of ocean seemed to tell.
>
> Teach me half the gladness
> that thy brain must know,
> Such harmonious madness
> From my lips would flow,
> The world should listen then, as I am
> listening now.
>
> *The Wanderer*, Eugene Field

Listening is an art and, like all other arts, it requires practice. Many can hear, but few have mastered the art of listening — a skill that is half the art of communicating.

In my own early life, listening was not always a pleasure and certainly not a method I employed in the performance of my duties. In fact, I recall that, during my childhood, my mother would frequently admonish me to "Just listen!" So easy, and yet so difficult.

Some athletes with whom I have spoken feel that coaches seem to have special difficulty with the practice of listening. Perhaps so many people want to listen to them that coaches become preoccupied with the questions posed to them and lose the sense of their own need to listen.

Examples of Listening

I try to practice the art of listening during my annual pilgrimage to the NCAA basketball finals—one of the great joys of my coaching life. At the conclusion of every basketball season, the Final Four tournament serves, like dessert, to wash out the taste of a frustrating season or to add a touch of sweetness to a fulfilling one. There I hear the sounds of knowledgeable coaches exchanging tales in the hotel lobby, sounds of anger in the stormy meetings on rule changes, clinicians voices filtering from rooms where strategies are developed, and ground-swell sounds of excitement rising to fever pitch as the last seconds tick away in the final game. The joy I find in the Final Four sessions is due, in no small measure, to the opportunities they provide to listen.

In the summer between my junior and senior years of college, I was one of a large contingent of Air Force ROTC cadets at James Connally Air Force Base in Waco, Texas, for four weeks of orientation to Air Force life. One day all the cadets traveled to Fort Hood, forty to a bus, to see jet fighters strafe simulated enemy tanks. In the bus in which I was riding were 38 male cadets. Two women Air Force personnel (WAFS) sat together on a front seat. As boredom began to set in on the hot, dusty ride to Fort Hood, some of the troops began to sing. They sang familiar tunes at first, but, as time wore on, the merriment turned into raucous vulgarity—much to the embarrassment of the lady officers. The sounds had changed.

One of the cadets on the bus was Howard "Hopalong" Cassady, the fleet-footed Ohio State halfback who won the Heisman Trophy in 1956. Cassady listened for a while, but his neck reddened as the singing turned lewd. When it seemed that the tone would not change, he stood in the aisle and shouted over the din, "That's enough!" You could have heard a pin drop for the remainder of the trip. It was a brave and righteous act.

All aboard the bus heard the nasty refrains, but only Cassady was able to listen and to apply a reasoned response to what he heard. Unlike hearing, listening requires concentration on the sound and judgement of its applicability to the listener before a behavioral response can occur.

Music and Nature

It has been said that music is the spirit of the soul. People march to music, dance to music, even study to music. It sets a mood. It is often invigorating, strengthening, motivating. Some of my own teams have found that the cords of marching music lends an uplifting spirit before a game.

Nature, too, offers sounds to excite our sensitivities. Every summer I go to Tobey Hill in New Hampshire. There is a place there on a moss-covered knoll — hidden by wolf pines, bursting with lady slippers — where I go to listen. What I hear is the music of the wind rustling through the pine boughs, the chickadees serenading each other in turn, and, in the evenings, the echo-like calls of the whip-poor-wills. And, from that place of quietude, I also re-hear words of counsel spoken 30 years ago by my father, the promises I made to my wife at our wedding, and even the sounds of exploding anti-aircraft fire over embattled marines in Manila during the waning days of World War II.

Moments of aloneness force us to absorb the messages of the sights and sounds around us, even those of yesteryear.

Solitude

Places of solitude and times for aloneness scheduled into the routine of our lives present opportunities to listen, to ponder, to reflect on the day-to-day happenings of our lives. They allow us to measure our feelings, our words, and our actions.

The Fellowship of Christian Athletes, an organization embracing athletes, coaches, and others interested in the development of richness in life, has come under attack from some coaches who suggest that the "do-gooders" take the necessary meanness out of potentially strong young athletes. I have never found that to be true. And the Fellowship provides a particularly useful experience for young men and women — that of the quiet time scheduled into each day's agenda at every FCA summer conference. That block of time underscores the importance of reflection about self — self in relation to others, self in relation to a greater being, and self in relation to goals. I have marvelled at the magnificent growth experienced by those who have gone through such reflection, and I therefore endorse this or a similar form of "time-to-listen" practice for all prospective coaches. These practices can help bring some order into coaches' lives and reason into their decision making.

I have also seen transformations occur in the lives of adult campers sharing in what is known as the Wahcondah hour at a summer camp in New England. The hour provides an occasion for absolute stillness in order to reflect, to listen, in an environment of hills, fields, rocks, and ponds framed with sunrises and sunsets. The opportunity quietly to savor the goodness in the birds of the air, the flowers of the field, and the stir of the branches in a fresh breeze is a rich one.

In Kyoto, Japan, I have been witness to transformations brought about by the Zazen experience of Zen worshippers. Zazen worshippers sit in the stoic starkness of a bare room, seated on a *tatami* with legs crossed, often facing a wall for one or two hour periods broken only by a slow, ritual walk once around the small room. Aside from testing one's physical flexibility, the experience forces a milieu of stillness in which real listening can occur.

The Story of Martha and Mary

Readers of the scriptures may be familiar with the passage in the book of *Luke* describing the inspiration derived from listening. As it is written, Jesus and his followers interrupt their travel to stop at the home of Martha and Mary, who set about preparing dinner for the group. As Martha hustles about the kitchen watching over several cooking pots and simultaneously preparing dishes and refreshments, she notices her sister, Mary, sitting in the next room listening to their guests talk. Exploding in anger, Martha says to Jesus: "Doesn't it make any difference to you that I'm here in the kitchen doing all the work alone? Tell my sister to get out here and help!" Jesus responds by saying that Mary is doing the truly important thing in listening to the conversations. Luke seems to be telling readers that there is more to the good life than the constant business of hard work. There comes a time when the greater good is simply in listening.

Listening and Coaching

For students of coaching, and even for those of us who have coached for decades, listening takes on more technical importance when related to professional clinics and workshops. The clinics I have attended number in the hundreds, but I can't recall one in which I didn't learn something important to my professional life by listening to the various speakers. I regret that I did not develop the practice of attending these enclaves even while an undergraduate. Attending clinics and listening to the speakers seems to me today to be a useful assignment for students preparing to be professional coaches. Like physicians who must attend seminars to remain abreast of changes in their medical practices, coaches must similarly make time to absorb the sounds at professional workshops where masters share their knowledge if they hope to keep up with the advancement and increasing complexity of their specialty sports.

Coaches are very often approached by members of their teams while at home or in their offices. I have discovered that, normally, there rests behind these visits a desire to share a concern. Coaches should recognize those concerns. These are good times to listen.

One time, a coach who was confronted by a player with a perplexing problem replied, "My line is coaching. Take that nonsense to a shrink." The response may serve well as a humorous after-dinner story. But, in reality, it did nothing to salve the sores of a heavy-hearted young person — someone who understandably expected his coach to care and to listen.

The coaching profession requires of its leaders that they be tough-minded, but it also demands tender-heartedness. The art of listening compromises neither and wins lasting respect.

Listening is an art. Develop it. The mastery of the art will lend immeasurably to coaching effectiveness.

50 OFF THE BENCH

9
DEALING WITH ADVERSITY
a case of lack of luck?

> No matter how they twist and wind
> It's you and I who make our fates.
> We open up or close our gates
> On the road ahead or the road behind.
> Moriarty

When I was growing up, one of the popular songs was entitled *Qué Sera*. It had a catchy tune and even now I sometimes find myself humming the bobbing notes. However, I have always been skeptical of the message in the words, "Whatever will be, will be. The future's not ours to see...." Fatalistically, these words describe a world unmanageable, a life uncontrollable, a sort of pre-arranged destiny for each of us. They are downright scary! I would much prefer to believe that within us exist the resources to have some control over our lives. I shudder to think how dreadful I would feel if all the adversities encountered in life had to be accepted as matters of bad luck or fate and could not be dealt with through reason. Such pessimism!

How often we have heard the pre-game exhortation "Good luck" and the post-game explanations "We were lucky" or "The ball just took an ill-fated bounce." Coaches use the term "luck" more than occasionally — often to place blame for the outcomes of games on forces beyond their control. But can victories or defeats be that easily attributed to luck?

As youngsters at summer camp we used to sing a song about four-leaf clovers — one leaf for hope, one leaf for faith, another for love, and the last one for luck. But, as the song later points out, one must *search* to find where the four leaf clover grows. That we must search indicates that we can have at least a partial control over our destinies.

From my experience, it seems that good fortune most frequently accompanies those who have toiled the hardest. As Dave Strack, the former University of Michigan basketball coach once said, "Good luck occurs where preparation and opportunity meet." It might be easier for coaches whose professional lives are strewn with difficult hurdles to shrug off responsibility for all outcomes and blame destiny, but it isn't honest.

Two Inspiring Women

Many people have been heroic in rising above adversity. When Beethoven had become completely deaf, he continued to compose music, and John Milton reportedly wrote some of his greatest works of poetry after he had gone blind. However, when I find myself fretful over misfortune and tempted to attribute my disappointments to luck or some other fatalistic demon, I turn my thoughts to two wondrous ladies who through perseverance, hard work, and a perpetual optimism have learned that adversity need not be accepted without question — that it can be overcome.

One of these women I met in Calcutta. The most hopeless feeling I have ever experienced (outside of once having vainly tried my skills in a one-on-one basketball game with John Havlicek) was in walking through the central market of downtown Calcutta. I have been to many open markets in this world from Tegucigalpa to Shanghai and Dar Es Salaam, but none possess Calcutta's sensual extremes. In the deadly heat and humidity of the delta region, the combined aromas of dead fish, rotting eggs and vegetables, and human and cattle excrement seem to penetrate every nerve ending. Even the flies and rats seem larger in Calcutta. But in the midst of all this walks each day a small, slightly stooped lady, her tanned and weathered face the only hint of her advanced years.

On the day we met, she wore a light blue habit trimmed in white, the traditional garb of the Sisters of Charity. Seating herself next to me in the near vacant waiting room of the Dum Dum Airport in the sultry dawn hours, Mother Theresa began to converse in quiet tones about a program of mosquito control that she hoped would lessen the incidence of malaria among Indian children. She spoke also of a program to relocate the orphaned children of the area to healthier environments throughout the world. Her entire countenance radiated hope. Each thought was expressed with a determined optimism.

Qué Sera — phooey! The power of Theresa, so rich in goodness for humankind, lies in the belief that every obstacle obstructing her work can and will be conquered. At no point in our conversation did this selfless little nun speak in terms of *if*. Rather she said, "*When* we convince government of the urgency to succeed in this endeavor, then will our children be free." She so believed in the miracle of achievement for the poverty stricken of the world that listeners, too, become buoyed with a spirit of hope and optimism.

Parting from her, I wished her luck in her work. As though to redirect my concern, she replied, "Thank you for your prayers."

The other woman in my acquaintance whose deeds have served as a frequent reminder on how to deal with adversity is Rachel Saint.

"This will work," she said to me aboard a small aircraft flying over the jungles near Limon Cocha, the base camp for the Wycliffe Missionary Translators in Eastern Ecuador. She was outlining her plan, hatched years earlier, to safely enter the Auca tribe encampment on the Napo River, in order to help the Aucas develop a written language.

Her plan was to put microphones on the wingtips of a helio-airplane that would circle over a village of thatched huts along the river. The microphones would be used, she explained, to record the vocal sounds of the shouting group of cannibalistic Aucas who would gather along the river, as usual, at the sound of an approaching craft.

Saint eventually put her plan into action. From the recordings, she was able to piece together words, and this eventually led to her courageous first contact with the migrant Indians.

Saint's own brother, Nate, and his party of five had been speared to death several years earlier by the same natives as they had attempted a similar encounter. In light of this, Saint's own optimism was laudatory. She never wavered from the belief that, though difficult and dangerous, such contact was both possible and necessary. The odds of success were as long as the Aucan spears, and she was often advised to abandon her goals. But Saint overcame each obstacle in her path and set about the task determinedly.

In the years since that in-flight meeting with Miss Saint, the world has come to know of her successful efforts in translating the Auca tongue into the written word. Through Saint's caring, the Aucas have also come to lead more civilized, less war-like lives. Again, *Qué Sera* — phooey!

The works of these two women serve as ongoing reminders that a bold and daring forthrightness can overcome adversity. These women provide inspiring examples of perseverance for all of us. They responded to need's call and allowed true spirit to dominate their lives — with dramatic results.

Adversity and Coaching

Coaches would do well to heed the examples of Mother Theresa and Rachel Saint, to catch their selfless spirit, and to reach out, despite adversities, to the athletes so dependent on their example.

In my own coaching life, I have on many occasions felt like the deprived waifs on the streets of Calcutta. This has been especially so during the throes of seasons made grievous by injury, defections, defeats, and job pressures.

Often, the trumpet sound put forth by coaches experiencing such misfortunes has a familiar, pessimistic ring. How frequently we hear coaches make self-protecting and gloomy predictions as a means of warding off potential criticisms. "If we can escape injury, we should be ok", or "If we get through this part of the schedule with our heads above water, maybe we can win a game," or "We will be lucky to come out of this game alive." They go on and on. I know most of the standard lines of woe, because I have used many of them in my own coaching life.

Projections of this sort can at times relieve the pressures on young teams, but their overuse reminds me of the story about the little boy who too often cried "Wolf." People simply paid no heed after recognizing the invalidity of the alarm.

Students of coaching need to recognize that the profession lives with adversity. Without it the challenges so attractive to many who enter the field would not exist. Without adversity, in fact, the profession might even be boring (although such "boredom" has sometimes been welcomed by those wearied by the pressures and toils).

Some coaches thrive on adversity. Others make strong efforts to keep adversity from the door, fearful that it's ultimate outcome will shorten or destroy their careers. But — regardless of whether adversity is sought out, avoided, or dreaded — it will never go away. Adversity in some form is a given that always accompanies the coaching life. It is a part of the business, and coaches are best served by accepting the inevitable variety of calamities. In accepting distressing events as given factors in a big equation, coaches can reasonably and optimistically move forward toward the fulfillment of their goals.

10
FOREIGN TRAVEL
a treasure trove of ideas

> Travel, in the younger sort, is a part of education; in the elder, a part of experience.
>
> Francis Bacon

No longer can coaches meet the expectations of those with whom they work without a constant effort to search for new truths that can add new dimensions to their labors. As neurosurgeons must grow with new developments in their field, so must coaches grow with new developments in athletics. And in this world, constantly made smaller by technological advancement, travel provides a viable source of growth for coaches — a time for broadening themselves.

Judging from some conversations I have had in recent years, I would say that many coaches persist in the belief that everything to be learned about the fundamentals of sports can be found somewhere between Fort Kent, Maine, and San Diego, California. Even those who admit that American coaches can occasionally profit from glimpses at European practices rarely recognize the lessons to be learned from Asia or from Third World nations in Africa and South America. "East is least and West is best" sometimes seems to me more than a just the slogan used by fans of Columbus West High School when hosting their Columbus East rivals.

But there is in fact a great deal to be learned from sporting practices in other countries. Indeed, if American coaches fail to recognize other nations' methods as potentially useful for the betterment of their own programs, we may face the day when athletic achievement in the West will rest while the feasts belong to the East.

Even if a coach witnesses no athletic practices during an overseas experience, the change of living pattern from the usual routine of coaching life yields fantastic rewards in new vigor and fresh perspectives.

My Own Experience

In my collegiate coaching career, I have taken four leaves of absences. The first centered in Ecuador, South America, and was conducted under the joint auspices of the Peace Corps and Heifer Project. My work varied from assisting a family-planning physician in remote Indian villages of the Andes Mountains to the presentation of basketball coaching workshops in the capital city of Quito.

Three years later, on a mini-leave, I spent a term teaching a basketball coaching class to a group of Filipino coaches at Silliman University on Negros Island. It was during this leave that I developed a fascination with snorkeling in the coral-laden waters of the inland seas.

Most recently, my family and I shared a second leave in Japan, teaching and advising club-sports programs at International Christian University near Tokyo. The concentrated study in Japanese language and history we have undertaken during these leaves has developed into another area of personal interest.

One return trip from Japan took three months and carried us through 23 countries in Asia and Europe. On this sojourn, I conducted basketball clinics in India and Tanzania.

My own — very subjective — judgement of these experiences is that, at the very least, they have given me a new perspective on the world and that they broadened me personally. I also believe that, as a result of these experiences, I have been able to bring new dimensions to my work — dimensions that have made me a better coach and a better teacher.

A list of the discoveries I have made in my travels abroad would fill a book by itself. Here I will offer a few examples of foreign sports practices that might be useful for American coaches.

Sumo and Tennis in Japan

Before my sabbatical leaves in Japan, I — like many other Westerners — conceived of *sumo* wrestling as a sport in which two big-bellied behemoths engaged in a stomach-bumping contest until one was shoved from the ring. *Sumo* combatants *are* generally large men (some well in excess of six feet and 400 pounds), but many are extremely agile as well as strong. And *sumo*, the "sport of emperors," is a colorful spectacle, involving centuries-old traditions with religious overtones.

Included in the ceremony is a period in which the rivals strut several times from the starting position at the ring's center to containers of salt in their respective corners. Each takes a handful of salt and tosses it across the circle. This practice, the origins of which lie in the Shinto religion, has as its object the purification of the combat area.

The wrestlers also engage in psychological interplay using techniques such as staring, grimacing, and slapping of thighs to "act" on their opponents and pump themselves up.

The average bout lasts about 10 seconds—about the same as a football play. The clash itself resembles the head-to-head conflict of a couple of professional football linemen. In fact, football coaches might do well to have linemen and linebackers emulate *sumo* throws in their drills. Viewings of *sumo* spectacles would, I'm certain, make coaches more imaginative when formulating drill concepts for their football programs.

Sean Sloane, a college tennis coach and a referee of professional tennis tournaments, has already borrowed a method from the Japanese—a method for cleaning court lines during side-changes. To provide a cleared area on which linespersons can easily see ball impressions on clay tennis courts, the Japanese run a roll brush behind the various boundary lines. Sloane has adopted this practice for state-side tournaments. He has also borrowed from the Japanese the idea of using teenagers to make line calls at professional tournaments, proving that young eyes and quick reflexes can make for good judgements. The reputation of line-calling at Japanese tournaments is widely acclaimed by professional players as the best on the world circuit.

Travels in China

Even travel through China in all its ancient ways, an experience I compare to a ride in a time capsule, offers something of importance to athletic coaches.

The Chinese use of acupuncture in relieving muscle and joint pain has long been acknowledged in the western world. It seems that the techniques are successful, but sadly little is known of their potential applicability to our own athletic-injury problems.

American coaches would also benefit from study of Chinese sports training methods. Observing a school program in women's volleyball in Nanking reminded me of some of the "torture tests" reportedly used by the ancient Spartans in developing toughness and maximizing pain thresholds. Practicing without the ball, the teenage girls in these skirmishes would hurl their bodies to the hard clay, even to the point of being bloodied and bruised. The practice conforms to the Chinese tradition of total dedication to perfection. Small wonder that these toughened athletes frequently up-end their bigger western counterparts in international volleyball competition!

Basketball in the Himalayas

In Mussoorie, a Tibetan refugee village high in the Indian Himalayas, I watched the area's equivalent of high school regional championship basketball games. Fundamentals as we know them in the United States were sorely wanting in the play of all teams. I could not imagine college recruiters offering these lads inducements to play on American college teams. Yet, much could be learned from these mountain people about post-game conduct. The games were bitterly fought, and there was all the excitement and crowd noise that one would find in a high school gymnasium in Terre Haute, Indiana. But, at the conclusion of the games, each player from the losing team sought out a counterpart from the victorious team, hugged him, raised the victor's hand high in the air, and marched him around the court in a display of humility which was appreciated by the crowd. Deeply moved, I recognized this as a gesture that could well be borrowed in our efforts to develop sportsmanship in our own young athletes.

Volleyball in Ecuador

In the small villages high in the Andes mountains of Ecuador, the favorite sport is volleyball — mountain style. Indian men challenge all comers for Sucres (the local currency) on clay surfaces with a single rope strand strung across the court for a net. The rope is strung at the nine foot level, a foot higher than international standards. Placing the "net" at that height makes spiking nearly impossible, thereby putting a great premium on making drop shots and placement of the ball. Playing with just three people on a side at altitudes up to 12,000 feet makes the game an outstanding conditioner. Often games are played with a ball that is little more than a kapok-filled, hand-sewn, burlap bag. But no other volleyball games anywhere are conducted with greater enthusiasm and excitement.

Training in Tanzania

Dean Smith, John Thompson, and other basketball coaches might do well to book an excursion to East Africa, not just to recruit the budding talent in that area of the world, but to observe some training methods of the young athletes there. On a leave from Williams College, I conducted basketball workshops on the outdoor courts of Dar Es Salaam. I was awed by basketball hopefuls shinnying up coconut-palm trees to increase thigh, calf, and upper-body strength. And jumping rope on the white-sand beaches near Dar Es Salaam is acclaimed locally as the finest routine for developing power jumping ability. These methods seem crude compared to the use of modern weight contraptions in America, but they are carried out with full enjoyment and a frolicsome spirit — and one can't argue with the results!

※ ※ ※ ※ ※

Frequently, coaches who concur that foreign travel holds great potential for joy and growth go on to explain why they cannot do it. Some offer that the schools or universities at which they teach won't give them leaves for travel. Some say that they cannot allow themselves to miss a coaching season because of the damage their absence would do to their program. And some suggest that they just cannot afford foreign travel.

There is no question that something is lost with almost every gain, but the balance must be closely weighed. As I have suggested, coaches can learn much from foreign travel and they can "recharge" themselves so that they can take up their coaching duties with renewed vigor. If there is real conviction that these rewards outweigh the losses, ways can often be found to get over the hurdles, especially with the wide variety of subsidized programs sponsored nowadays by organizations around the country.

11
CHANGING JOBS
a prescription for perspective

> Our deepest obligations...are to be maladjusted to the *status quo*....We cannot save this world without changing it,...we cannot save our economic system without changing it, [and] we cannot save ourselves without being changed, radically changed, transformed by the renewing of our minds.
>
> Harry Emerson Fosdick

Among coaches, the subject of changing jobs unearths a spectrum of reactions — from the bitterness of one who has been forced to change jobs to the elation of one who has fulfilled a dream by being hired to a select coaching position.

Commitments

In recent years, the coaching profession has come under deserved criticism for the rather cavalier manner in which coaches — especially at the college and professional levels — have broken contractual commitments to institutions. In great numbers, coaches are seeking and finding positions without regard for the agreements they have previously made.

Worse, some noted universities and professional organizations have enticed coaches known to be under contract to other institutions. Professional leagues have rules that are supposed to prevent this behavior, but the rules don't always have the intended effect.

Hooray, then, for Angelos Drossos, former owner of the Spurs, San Antonio's professional basketball franchise. Following a successful season by his team, Drossos spoke out against attempts to lure away his coach, Stan Albeck, who was under contract. Drossos said that he would not grant any team an audience with Albeck and that he would consider it an "insult" if any team sought one. (Still, the system won out. Albeck jumped contract and signed with New Jersey.)

Coaches have always deplored the disrespect shown them by administrators who recklessly release coaches to satisfy interest groups. But coaches do little to deserve greater respect when they sever their contracts in pursuit of more promising ventures. The practice of breaking contracts, in most circumstances, is not appropriate for men and women whose lives serve as models for the young.

Also, coaches would do well to be more open about job hunting intentions. When the process of change is initiated through phone calls, submissions of resumes, or formal application, the authorities at the institution of current employment should be informed. This courtesy would eliminate the hard feelings that can develop when moves are discovered second-hand or through rumor. It would also indicate that, despite having the desire for job change, the coach has a sense of loyalty to and respect for the institution and coaching colleagues. A quick way to burn one's bridges and so leave a scar on one's professional reputation is to hunt for jobs surreptitiously.

Considerations of Philosophy

Fortunately, most job changes are voluntary, timed to the mutual satisfaction of coach and institution, and made for useful purposes. The rest of this chapter will center on considerations useful to coaches in search of new jobs, or those in the process of change.

One of the foremost of these considerations is whether the new institution's philosophy of sport is compatible with that of the coach. Coaches need to ask of themselves whether the institution of choice would allow the coach full latitude to pursue his or her coaching goals. Do the administrators to whom the coach would be immediately responsible pursue similar goals? Are they supportive in the way the coach would wish? To avoid disillusionment and unhappiness, a coach considering a job change should seek clear answers to these questions.

Often, the answers can be discovered by talking directly with coaches, administrators, and students. Sometimes answers can even be discovered by talking with people outside the institution who have knowledge of past practices. And occasionally written material that includes philosophical statements or descriptions of an athletic department's objectives may give insight into an institution's direction.

Few irritations are as grating in the life of a coach as the discovery that the philosophical aims of the school to which a commitment has been made are at odds with those that the coach supports. Prior to making a job change, coaches should use all available resources to inform themselves on the important matters of institutional philosophy.

Economics

Second in importance to philosophy but often first on a coach's mind is the economics of a proposed move. Will the change improve the quality of the coach's life through increased salary or other benefits? Will the new employer pay the cost of the move? Will the new employer provide adequate financial support for a program of the type the coach envisions?

In order to avoid misunderstandings, it is advisable to have all negotiated matters relating to economics outlined in a written contract or in some other formal document. Often verbal promises made in good faith are misconstrued as they pass from one desk to another in the bureaucratic chain of command.

Once, my own failure to follow the above advice resulted in embarrassment and in the loss of a low-interest college housing loan that I had negotiated in good faith with a dean about to go on sabbatical leave. When I tried to complete the house purchase, I was informed by a stand-in administrator that, due to several provisions in the college's loan policy, my application for a loan had been rejected. Everything worked out favorably in the end, but much anxiety could have been prevented if the results of the original negotiations had been spelled out initially with clarity and in writing.

Timing

Another consideration that should be taken into account by coaches thinking about job changes is timing. What effect will the move have on family affairs or on the children's education? Has service at the present institution been so short that the move might be labeled opportunistic?

One young college basketball coach, eager to raise his coaching status, has held five coaching positions at five universities in the past six years. This has necessitated five moves and the purchase of five homes — quite an upheaval for his wife and two children. And there is also a professional problem with transience of this sort. Potential employers are understandably apprehensive about hiring a coach with such a peripatetic record.

The practice of "hedge-hopping" may be excusable for assistant coaches as they search for positions compatible with their professional goals, but it is less becoming for head coaches. In recent years, several notable head coaches have abandoned teams in the middle of rebuilding programs for more lucrative offers. This form of fickle rainbow-chasing does nothing to reinforce the image of coaches as educators.

Other Considerations

Not to be overlooked in discussions of job changing are changes made to restore hope or renew growth. Coaching is like any other job: circumstances sometimes enclose coaches and choke off their ability to serve effectively.

All of us have the potential to make errors of judgement or to get caught in departmental political webs. Also, jobs can stifle some coaches growth, confining them by preventing them from testing their talents to the fullest. Despite the best efforts to sidestep these traps, they can occasionally hold coaches hostage in jobs that no longer appeal to them, challenge them, or suit them. When this happens, the hope rests in change — change of roles within an institution, change of place of employment, or even change of occupation.

A colleague once advised me that "after ten years on the job you've overstayed your welcome and will probably need a new venue of employment to challenge the senses and the soul." I wouldn't go so far as to offer this advice as a rule for all. But coaches should be alert to the fact that change can be healthy — that it can open doors to individual growth.

✵ ✵ ✵ ✵ ✵

It is important for all coaches periodically to weigh their effectiveness in their current employment situations. It is also important for coaches to weigh their usefulness on the job against the effects of their job on family, health, and personal growth. Only with periodic, objective assessment of current roles can coaches avoid whimsical changes and the risk of becoming "rooted," complacent, or ineffective.

12
LEADERSHIP
a barometer of coaching effectiveness

Leadership and learning are indispensable to each other.
John F. Kennedy

While coaches agree that leadership in athletics is paramount to team successes, there is little agreement on what constitutes positive leadership. Therefore, rather than attempting to define leadership, I shall outline several of the coaching patterns which, in my experience, have reflected the presence of leadership in athletic programs.

Being Forthright

Foremost in leadership qualities in coaching must be forthrightness. Coaches cannot be evasive in their relationships with players. Respect for a coach never diminishes more rapidly than when the coach offers weak, dishonest, or deceptive explanations in response to students' requests for information on matters of concern to them.

Abraham Lincoln, often cited for his qualities of leadership, credited his wife Mary for reminding him to speak out boldly and honestly in public utterances. During the latter days of the Civil War, a sense of death hung over the nation like a heavy blanket, and the country cried out for an explanation for the heavy losses of life. Tense and apprehensive two days before he was to deliver a public statement on the subject, Lincoln asked his wife what he should say. Her reply: "Tell them, Abraham, what the war is all about." He did just that, and the result was the now famous Gettysburg Address.

No grander example of forthright leadership has been evident in this generation than that displayed by Dr. Martin Luther King, chief spokesman and strategist for the Civil Rights movement. In the course of a few years, his following grew to millions and his message struck the very conscience of America. And in large part, King's success at leadership, like Lincoln's, was due to a forthrightness that left no doubts about his goals for a better American society.

Remaining Flexible

If a coach is to lead well, the coach must be amenable to technical, organizational or strategical change when it is called for.

Some coaches' success rests, at least in part, on their ability to change. Henry Iba, the former United States Olympic team basketball coach, was a master technician when it came to altering defenses, tempo, and styles of attack to match changes in personnel and to counter tactical changes by the opposition. Yet many coaches I have known, are set in their ways and resistant to change. Some university coaches even experience anxiety over the annual arrival of fresh faces into their programs, since the new students — coming from different athletic backgrounds and having different styles, goals, and expectations — bring with them the threat of forcing coaches to make changes in their systems.

Coaches who were active during the student unrest that was generated by race riots in the cities and by uneasiness about the draft and the war in Vietnam recall some of the radical changes that the upheaval around them thrust into their athletic programs. Many athletes, especially blacks, carried political messages into the athletic arenas by refusing to conform to common, traditional practices. And many coaches refused to acquiesce to student demands, staking out instead a position of intransigence.

I recently heard of a preacher who decided to move to a new parish. When he announced to his congregation that Jesus had called him to another church ministry, the congregation rose in unison and sang "What a Friend We Have in Jesus." Clearly, during the tenure of his ministry at that parish, that preacher must not have maintained sufficient flexibility to keep in touch with the sentiments of his congregation.

When coaches fail to keep abreast of what is current and refuse to consider, for example, putting in some new plays or drills, they can expect a similar response from their "faithful flock." Coaches should make every effort to ensure periodic "keeping in touch" experiences with those close to their programs. Such a practice will keep them informed and thus boost their leadership potential immensely.

Keeping Things in Perspective

Another important leadership trait is the ability to give highest priority to what is truly important. Too often coaches tend to "spin their wheels" on issues lacking in substance or projects that have only image value. It is easy sometimes to become mired in the multitude of distractions that accompany the coaching life and seem to surround athletic teams. When this happens, athletes often do not get the direction they need.

The late Branch Rickey was a man known for devoting his time and energies to important matters. Bored with trifles, he exerted himself vigorously in the cause of racially integrating professional baseball. His leadership is proof positive that, although inspiration amounts to little by itself, inspiration that results in relevant action can alter lives, teams, and even societies.

Because coaching is consuming work, there is a tendency for coaches to forget the needs of the very people who are the direct recipients of their efforts. Effective coaching leaders must assess the importance of each game and appraise the demands they should make on team members in preparation for the game.

I'm not suggesting that coaches deprive contests of all intensity or that they make fewer demands on students. What I am suggesting is that greater emphasis be placed on long-term, people-developing goals than on game-oriented goals. The balance of goals usually is favorable when the coaches involved in game preparation have succeeded in infusing the participants with the desire to excel.

Coaches who raise emotional levels to a high pitch for each game do not benefit their teams in the long run. More substantive, long-term goals become lost in programs that reach game-outcome goals through emotional means. For instance, anger stirred up in an athlete for a game sometimes overflows onto the athlete's teammates or family after the game is over. Coaches whose leadership centers on fomenting anger to stimulate performance are like contractors building a home on quicksand: They lack good judgement, and their product is fragile. The goals of a leader-coach will not be limited to preparation for tomorrow's game. Rather the leader-coach will develop long-term goals, which hold richer rewards for individual development and, in themselves, will raise the quality of play for each game. In basketball lore, John Wooden of UCLA most noticeably brought out these leadership traits.

In stressing the importance of keeping sports in proper perspective, I am reminded of a statement made by Kevin McHale of the Boston Celtics about the leadership qualities of his former coach, K. C. Jones:

> When [Jones] says something once, he doesn't have to say it twice. Our former coach used to yell at us so much that sometimes you'd tune it out, start doing something else. When K. C. yells, everybody sits up and listens.

Young coaches should be cautious not to assume that the only leadership models are those so often visible on television or at courtside—blustery, effusive, arm-waving screamers attempting, like jockeys, to ride home winners. Clearly, personalities vary widely among effective leaders.

The true leaders are those coaches who view their sport as something constructive for the participants — something that can foster growth of personality, a means to a bigger end. Like drivers on the Los Angeles freeways who must ever be aware of what is happening behind, beside, and in front of them, the best coaches have their heads on swivels; they constantly assess and re-assess the direction of their programs in light of the growth of the students who are involved.

John Wooden has said,

> Certain sports can build character and they can just as quickly tear it down. It's not the sport itself, though, but the administration of the sport that can cause the problem. You've got to keep it in perspective, to make the players understand that outscoring someone in an athletic contest is not the greatest thing in the world and being outscored is not a terrible thing.

This is good counsel for coaches who aspire to be good, effective leaders. Coaches need to keep their antennae ever scanning, alert to their own vital needs and those of their athletes.

Nurturing Togetherness

Some teams seem to have a spirit of camaraderie or togetherness. The members of these teams take genuine joy in one another's company, and they seem to give their all in every game if for no other reason than to retain the allegiance of their teammates.

Behind every such team, you can be certain, is a coach doing what is necessary to nurture team spirit. There are any number of ways that this can be done, once the coach has recognized its importance.

One recognized method for developing team closeness is by providing opportunities for team members to have time together away from the usual place of practice — for example, on a picnic, camp-out, or team trip. In a setting and context different from the ordinary, team members come to know and respect each other as people, and this is very important. For the players, time away from the practice field or court offers the opportunity to discover how their personalities fit into the puzzle that is the team. And, in these settings, a coach can more easily prevail on students to express their true feelings about team issues, rules, or procedures. Disciplines are established. Allegiances are built.

One of my most fulfilling seasons as a basketball coach followed a team excursion to Cuba, where we participated in exhibition contests against the Cuban national team. For the squad, the most important thing about the venture was that it provided the opportunity for twelve young men to interrelate with each other in hotels, on buses, on the beach, and in shops. Even their interaction on the basketball floor was different from usual, since the atmosphere of the games in international exhibitions carried fewer of the pressures than those of intercollegiate competitions. The trip was designed to promote good will and good times. Everybody played in the games, and the players' roles became more clearly defined.

Students fed off the "Cuba time" for the rest of the season. They had shared a common experience, unique to them, and this experience set them on a mental pedestal. There was good feeling.

Less extravagant but equally productive experiences can be created for most teams by imaginative coaches who accept their roles as leaders. To students, such experiences are symbolic. As a flag can stir a nation to action, so a venture of this kind can stir young people to create a sense of togetherness and of common resolve.

Being Loyal

Coaches often threaten their leadership roles by misusing the media. Nothing disturbs athletes more than to discover a coach's disloyal comments about them or their performances in a newspaper or to hear about such comments secondhand from friends. But scarcely a day goes by that there isn't a piece dwelling on a coach's negative comments about a player in the sports pages of most of the major newspapers around the country.

Little good comes from this form of leadership. Examples are rampant. After a recent loss, for instance, an eastern football coach called his players "babies" in an exchange with the media, and, when the players found out about it, they were incensed. Similarly, after a college coach was quoted in the newspapers as saying that the interceptions thrown by his quarterback were "silly, terrible, ridiculous passes," the infuriated quarterback reported that he wanted to transfer. Stories of this kind are realized all too frequently.

How easy it is for coaches to become calloused to the feelings of those for whom they are responsible! But coaches who try to lead their teams through glib interviews with the media lose sight of the meaning of their roles as coaches.

Frederick Pabst, the brewer who "made Milwaukee famous," once wrote, "Nothing nobler have I found on earth than faithfulness from the heart and quiet from the mouth." Certainly no people want more of themselves than performers and athletes, and no one feels worse about a poor performance than the one who gave it. So, little is gained by chastising a performer through public utterances.

Most coaches expect their players to be loyal to them. But some coaches need be reminded that, as leaders, they ought to react to student wants in the way they expect students to respond to theirs. Coaches are under a constant obligation to make their own lives models for students.

Unlike Olympic runners who win tangible gold medals, coaches are rewarded most by knowing that they have given their best to the players in their trust.

Leading in Defeat

Another aspect of coaching life that calls for strong leadership is showing young people how to win humbly and lose graciously.

On a number of occasions, I have walked into a locker room to see printed on the wall the common sports saying,

Winning isn't everything; it's the only thing.

Whenever I see this, especially in school environments, I feel nauseated. The saying, supposedly made by the great coach Vince Lombardi, has done more to misdirect coaching leadership in this country than anything else imaginable. In fact, the quotation is not accurate. Lombardi was a gracious loser, never lowering himself to making negative comments about players of either team after a defeat. What Lombardi actually said was,

> Winning isn't everything; the pursuit of winning is what is important.

There is a significant difference between the statement attributed to Lombardi and the one he actually made. Aspiring coaches would do well to notice this difference and to pay heed to the message that was in fact Lombardi's.

As Helen Keller suggested, "out of pain grow the violets of patience and sweetness." In sports, a world of possibilities grows out of defeat and adversity. If coaches can't lift young people out of the doldrums of defeat and confusion, their coaching will be in vain, because defeat in some form is a part of every young athlete's life. Coaches who lead well do not leave players in the ashes; they optimistically seek out ways to inspire them and rebuild confidence after every setback.

Being Responsible Teachers

I will touch on one other area related to leadership in coaching that is vitally important but often overlooked: the coach's responsibility as a teacher.

Widespread, spontaneous interest in sports gives coaches a large advantage over teachers in other departments of high schools, colleges, and universities. Whatever faculty in academic disciplines may think about the educational merit of athletics, none can deny the sincerity and vigor of the student enthusiasm for it. Indeed, the students of teacher-coaches seem to possess an inexhaustible supply of zest and excitement that arouses the envy of teachers of academic subjects. Many academicians would consider themselves lucky if they could arouse even a fraction of the interest displayed by the most languid candidates for athletic teams. That this boundless interest and enthusiasm is placed under coaches' control puts upon them a large responsibility and offers them a magnificent educational opportunity.

Modern educational theory emphasizes the importance of making students feel that assignments are tasks they are privileged, rather than obliged, to do. This attitude, which teachers in academic subjects can create only through intense effort, is natural on the playing field or court. The educational value of sports can therefore be easily realized. The challenge facing coaches is that of fully appreciating their responsibility to bring to the athletic laboratory the fodder on which eager minds can feed.

Too many coaches, I have discovered, are tempted to ignore this educational responsibility, preferring to graze in the comfort of teaching "how to win." To focus fully on that, however, is to neglect the bigger lessons athletics have to teach. If we forget all else as leaders of young athletes, let us at least remember that the real effectiveness of our leadership is measured by the extent to which we make the athletic experience a fully educational one for our students.

13
RECRUITING
a path of thorns

> Whoever wants to know the heart and mind of America had better learn baseball, the rules and realities of the game — and do it by watching first high school or small-town teams.
> *God's Country and Mind*, Jacques Barzun

Talking about the talented basketball players who seem to grow in abundance like walnuts in the Kentucky hills, Adolph Rupp — the famed, former University of Kentucky coach — explained his recruiting strategy with a scriptural phrase: "I look to the hills from whence cometh my help."

While Rupp did not invent the practice of recruiting fine athletes, he did show what recruitment can produce in winning records and spinning turnstiles. Today the popularity of athletic programs at the major college level rests, in large measure, on the practice of wide-scale recruitment by coaches. The desires for personal acclaim and for program promotion through television revenue, commercial endorsements, alumni contributions, and gate receipts all serve as motivation for coaches' combing every hamlet in America, and even abroad, for the talent to produce winning teams.

Recruiting Malpractice

The obsession to win or to be Number One can be seen in almost every aspect of American life from beauty pageants to politics, and we often ignore rules that get in the way of realizing such favored status. Once, when riding along Massachusetts' Mohawk Trail, I noted a sign on the back of a septic-tank truck that read,

Joe's Septic System — We're #1 in the #2 business.

America's love affair with the status of being Number One, interestingly, extends even into such commercial enterprises.

In their zeal to secure the elusive Number One status or to insure top ratings with a win-at-all-costs approach to program development, coaches sometimes use extreme measures to win the hearts of "blue-chip" prospects. I have heard tell of one college coach who completely forgot to pick up a potential football recruit at the local bus station. The lad was disenchanted and hopped the next bus home. But, when the coach later realized his error, he wrote to the prospect as follows:

> Dear Ed,
> I'm very sorry for having missed you yesterday. I had been up all night. My wife was having a baby. I'm sorry to report that she had a girl instead of a boy, because I had intended to name him after you.

This note won the athlete over, and he later signed a letter of intent with the coach's university.

In recent days, coaches have taken even more aggressive recruiting measures, willfully violating NCAA regulations in their hot pursuit of athletic talent, and the escalating improprieties have cast a pall on the credibility of many educational institutions. Too many schools have gone so far as to prostitute their academic reputations by using unethical recruitment practices — practices tolerated, and even at times endorsed, by short-sighted administrators.

Former Celtic star, and college basketball coach, Bob Cousy, has bluntly spoken of recruiting malpractices. Said Cousy: "For at least 20 years now, recruiting practices in college basketball have been completely corrupt. When the example has been set by institutions, impressionable kids get the idea. Get the grade, get the votes, get to the top of the ladder-get the money."

Eddie Robinson, the highly respected football coach and athletic director of Grambling State University, cites widespread use of illegal recruiting practices. "What coaches are saying is 'I'll cheat and I'll beat the NCAA'," says Robinson. "The sense is that if they are not caught, then they are not cheating." The accusation is echoed by Bill Curry, the Kentucky football coach. "[Coaches] cheat, they're vicious, they're dishonest," Curry has said. "They will cheat and sacrifice young minds with drugs or whatever it takes to win." Similarly, in explaining why he resigned as the Creighton

University basketball coach, Willis Reed said, "If you're going to stay in college basketball and be successful, you'll have to do some things I can't do, I won't do. I know we've lost kids constantly because of it. I find down the line they have been offered things." Even Walter Byers, during his final year as Executive Director of the NCAA, expressed worry about recruiting abuses, and he challenged university presidents to address the problems on their own campuses.

The extent of recruiting malpractice is evidenced by the mounting numbers of university athletic programs under investigation by the NCAA. Several schools, slow to learn, have been placed on probation six or seven times in the past twenty-five years. Hopefully, recent NCAA legislation (called the "death penalty"), which calls for the two year suspension of programs found in violation twice within a five year period, will prove helpful.

The problem of athletic recruitment has the potential to destroy college sports as we have known them. Those of us interested in preserving athletic programs as educational programs within our universities, where virtue should reign, must fight the malaise in college sport caused by recruiting improprieties.

Athletics and Academic Standards

I have no quarrel with the thought that colleges can and should provide educational experiences for a wide variety of students — even for those whose likelihood for academic success is not great. However, I take issue with the pleas made by many coaches that their institutions lower admission standards to accommodate academic-risk students. The pleas of these coaches simply are not consistent with the realities of the programs offered by their schools. In fact, very few colleges adjust their curricula to provide viable academic experiences for poor-risk students — at least not to the extent that they ensure such adjustment all the way to graduation.

Noting this, some coaches, administrators, and legislators have suggested that athletics and academics should go their separate ways. Widely heralded in recent years has been the notion that institutions seeking high-powered, top-ranked teams should establish commercial teams under the universities' names and pay the athletes on those teams from gate receipts. One Nebraska legislator did, in fact, enter a bill into the Nebraska House of Representives that would have sanctioned the payment of Cornhusker athletes for their participation in sports.

Supporters of the plan note that it would put an end to the hypocritical practice of disguising pros-in-training as students, that it would allow academic institutions to uphold academic standards diligently, that it would allow for honest recruitment, and that it would increase opportunities for many who seek careers in professional sports. It has also been pointed out that, while the plan would loosen some of the ties between athletics and academia, it would not rule out the possibility that pros-in-training take some academic courses — such as courses in business — that might prove helpful to them in their careers. "Why should careers in athletics require an academic experience," supporters of the plan ask, "when other non-professional careers (masonry, carpentry, *etc.*) require only an apprenticeship?"

The primary argument offered by advocates of the plan, however, is that the present system of placing all college athletes into the mainstream of academic life doesn't work for all of the individuals being recruited. Too many do not fare well — a fact borne out by the alarmingly high percentage of student-athletes who do not graduate from college.

I feel, however, that for the vast majority of college athletes and for all of those at smaller, Division III institutions, the present practice of having academic requirements for athletic eligibility is the right one. Even among those college athletes who are interested in careers in professional sports, most lack the talent to pursue such careers. Statistics show that, for most, the thought that careers in professional sports will lead them to glory and wealth is simply an unrealistic dream. And the dream proves a disservice to many aspiring pros because it leads them into an academic curriculum of little substance. As one pro prospect said, "Why break my butt studying when I'm going to turn pro?" Student-athletes should be appraised of the facts and counselled to pursue educational training as though pro sports were not a career option.

Recruitment of academically unqualified student-athletes has prompted the structuring of watered down courses with little substance, sometimes taught by coaches themselves. Unfortunately, many of these courses, which aim at ensuring a passing performance, fall under the label "Physical Education," and serve the purposes of greedy coaches and others with athletic interests — *not* those of the student-athletes required to take them. At the other extreme, it is also unjust for student-athletes to be placed into demanding courses for which they are not prepared. Little wonder that many bored college athletes drop out of school even before their athletic eligibility has expired!

It seems to me that it would be beneficial for coaches to counsel athletes to dispel the fantasies of a life in the pros and to focus instead on a meaningful academic regimen. Even a "brush" with an academic experience would be more useful to most athletes than the "Mickey Mouse" courses subscribed to by some athletes and prescribed by their "academic advisers."

Rather than severing the ties between college-level athletics and academia, colleges committed to big-time athletic programs should develop preparatory courses to fit their students' needs, and they should provide *bona fide* tutors to help those student-athletes whose academic backgrounds are deficient.

Educational institutions wrong student-athletes by allowing those who are academically unqualified for the standard curricula into the system. Placing athletes who don't have the tools to succeed in an academically competitive atmosphere is comparable to putting a mouse in a cage with a boa constrictor! It is blatant exploitation of people for the use of their physical skills. Schools must either refuse to admit athletes who are academically unqualified or provide them with an opportunity to learn and grow at their own pace with specially developed but substantive courses.

Other Problems with Recruiting

The stresses on college athletes do not begin when they enter the classroom. A number of "blue-chip" prospects about whom much has been written have described the pressures brought to bear on them as they decided which college or university to attend. The *Los Angeles Times*, in reporting on the 1985 football recruiting classes of UCLA and USC, quoted Aaron Emanuel, a prospective student-athlete, on his feelings following the signing of a letter of intent to USC:

> I can sleep at night now. I thank God I didn't have a nervous breakdown through this thing. Tuesday was the first time I've smiled in a long time. I've been tense, but it feels as if I lost a thousand pounds off my back.

Another heavily recruited athlete once told me, "The experience of recruitment was stressful, especially when the coach started pressing for a decision. I almost got to the point of saying, 'I want out of this madness.' I even flirted with the idea of suicide!"

Typically, 18-year-olds are not equipped to cope with the attention heaped upon them by a multitude of newly found "friends," precious few of whom have the recruits' best interests in mind. The fact is that, in today's recruiting wars, a host of different people try to impose their selfish wishes on the decision-making process — reporters, agents, coaches, unseen messengers with "green-filled" envelopes, and even parents who have been made promises in return for their influence. Although all would swear that they are working in the prospects' best interest, the truth is that they most often bring confusion into the process of choice. Like parasites, they leave little breathing room for objective decision-making by the person whose life will be most affected.

The recruitment of "blue-chip" prospects also poses a danger to the prospects' self-image. By exalting athletes and their performances, coaches often give prospects a false sense of their importance and true talent level. The belief develops in some that they are owed more than the opportunity for an education. It is particularly difficult for recruits who have had attention constantly showered on them during the recruitment process to adjust to the harsh realities they face after they sign a letter of intent and, worse, after they report to campus for the beginning of their educational careers.

Also, when coaches or other interested parties try to "protect their recruited interests" — by altering academic records, overlooking illegal ticket sales by athletes, procuring "jobs" to supplement athletes' income, *etc.* — the efforts serve to reinforce the athletes' inflated ideas of their own importance.

All of that aside, it is sickening to see coaches, who are supposedly mature and dignified adults, drooling like a pack of starving coyotes at the doorstep of some hot-shot prep school prospect.

Sources of the Problem

In large part, the problems of the recruitment process arise from dependence of athletic programs on monies from gate receipts. Ultimately, if sport in America is really to be *sport*, institutions must find ways to keep athletic programs ticking without depending on "ticket money." If collegiate athletic programs are to be educational and, hence, worth retaining, their major source of funding must come from the operating budgets of the supporting institutions. Only in this way can faculties and administrators retain control. As long as gate receipts fund programs, coaches will be under pressure to keep their stadiums and gymnasiums filled. This in turn compels coaches to win games and, hence, to recruit "with no holds barred." As Rick Telander aptly phrased it in a *Sports Illustrated* article in October 1989, "As long as winning is the major concern, an endless flood of transgressions can be expected."

As more money pours into athletic coffers, there is more incentive for coaches to recruit with unethical abandon. Thus, sadly, some of the least profitable programs are also the cleanest.

Another source of problems for athletic programs at major colleges is the active participation in recruiting by groups not monitored or controlled by educational institutions: booster clubs, kickoff clubs, touchdown clubs, rebounder clubs, *etc*. When such organizations work only to promote institutional pride and to support various teams, they can be useful adjuncts to athletic programs. But, in some cases, these clubs actually manage aspects of athletic programs. Here problems arise. When power is placed in the hands of people who do not have to answer directly to an institution's or league's regulations, rules are violated, and the very integrity of a school may be jeopardized.

"Power tends to corrupt, and absolute power corrupts absolutely." These words of Lord Acton are appropriate to those of us concerned about the misuse of power in athletic support clubs. When booster groups conflict with institutional interests, philosophies, or goals — as too often happens — they should be disbanded.

Notre Dame's longtime guru of athletic interests, Father Edmund Joyce, has recognized the threat of booster clubs to athletic purity: "We don't have [a booster club]," he has said. "Abuses come that way. We've never wanted to start down that path." Perhaps Father Joyce's adherence to this policy accounts for his institution's remaining above the present rash of rules infractions involving recruitment of athletes.

Another, greater menace to collegiate sport is the ultra-loyalist fan who, perhaps in ignorance, places athletes and programs in compromising positions by offering "under the table" inducements to recruits. One NCAA investigator has suggested that many infractions of NCAA recruiting policies result directly from the acts of people who are either ignorant of policies or feel outside the jurisdiction of those policies. But, when infractions are brought to light, it is not these people who suffer. It is the athletes, coaches, and the educational institutions that suffer the penalties and endure the adverse publicity.

The unfortunate consequence of the problems generated by the winning-entertainment-money-recruiting syndrome is that athletes are frequently molded into people with inaccurate perspectives on service, morality, and sportsmanship. As Telander noted in the *Sports Illustrated* article I noted earlier, "[Athletes] are often unable to function appropriately in the real world until they learn new methods of behavior and thought." This is a sad commentary on the state of college athletic programs today.

Recommendations

What can be done to forestall the menacing trend toward wider ranging abuses in college athletic recruiting? I strongly recommend these measures:

First, the responsibility for initiating contact between prospective student-athletes and institutions should rest with high school administrators, counselors, coaches, parents, and the prospects themselves. These people know the athletes' academic goals and qualifications, and they therefore are best qualified to give direction to the athletes' education. The current practice of college coaches seeking out talented performers and pressuring them into college-choice decisions based on athletic rather than academic opportunity perpetuates the problem of unqualified student-athletes entering into inappropriate academic environments.

Second, all recruitment should be done on-campus. While at the campus, prospective students have the opportunity, at least, to develop a sense of the conditions under which they may spend their college years. On-campus recruiting would also release the families of prospective students from the onerous pressure exerted by recruiters who constantly visit their homes.

Finally, national associations of college and university Presidents should take a united stance in policing admission and recruitment practices within their institutions. As sordid wrongs have mounted in college sports, Presidents have too long been on the sidelines in silence or disclaiming their responsibilities. In reviewing their common problems, the Presidents may develop a greater awareness of malpractice, and they may also find new, positive ideas as to how athletic programs in educational institutions might somehow become, in themselves, *educational*. Unless they find such ways, the Presidents should sever all academic ties connecting the present, hypocritical, semi-professional athletic programs with the rest of academia. My sense is that they would discover that at the root of the problem lies an ever escalating obsession with winning and the status of a Nmber One ranking that must be blunted if recruiting reform is to be realized.

Fortunately, in 1984, an association called the Presidents' Commission of the NCAA did come into being. This group led the charge for reform in the

Special NCAA Convention called by the Commission in the summer of 1985. More assertive leadership of this sort is sorely needed.

Recruiting as we do, we can only lead asunder the beauty which our profession has the potential to develop. It is a tragic waste when we so enshrine winning and the dollars that accompany it that we recklessly blight the attitudes and values of young people.

A few voices within the coaching profession have suggested that the current trend toward commercialism and professionalism will lead to the eventual return of more pure amateurism in school sports. The thought seems to be that, if things get bad enough, they will start to get better by themselves. But the history of Ancient Greek and Roman societies shows that athletic systems in which profit dictates practice eventually crumble. It is my sincere judgement that any movement away from the concept of sport for the sake of *education* at our institutions will destroy for most the real joys to be found in athletic participation.

14
PROGRAM PROMOTION
a need for deliberation

> American football is an occasion at which dancing girls, bands, tactical huddles and television commercial breaks are interrupted by short bursts of play.
>
> London Times

Views are varied on the extent to which scholastic athletic programs should engage in promotion — the long-standing practice of selling or popularizing teams by advertising them or seeking financial support for them. At one pole are administrators who take the position that one cannot beat the drum hard or often enough in the name of school sports programs. At the opposite pole are those of the "no type, no hype" school who say that, since sports programs are developed for students, the course of a particular program should be dictated only by the extent of student interest in it. Somewhere between these extremes is the view of the majority of educators— that, while promotion must have its limits, programs must be made attractive if they are to succeed.

But should programs practice the hard-sell or the soft-sell in promotion? Ultimately, coaches' personalities and philosophies, and perhaps even institutional policies or procedural demands, will dictate the proper style of program promotion, if promotion is to occur at all.

Positive Aspects of Promotion

For many years the young, energetic, enthusiastic, and resourceful boys' basketball coach at a high school in a rural, southern Ohio town was an advocate of the promotional hard-sell. This coach advertised his program vigorously, and, within a short time, the entire community got caught up in a swell of excitement over the basketball team — not unlike the scenes depicted in the film *Hoosiers*. Young boys and their parents dreamed of future glory on the high school team. Parent committees were organized for almost everything, including the sale of popcorn at home games, the procurement of advertisers for game programs, and even the splicing of the highlight film to be viewed at booster club meetings. The legion of volunteer parents even supervised particulars such as the style of the cheerleading costumes and the slogans for bumper stickers.

The team developed into a power in Ohio small school competition, advanced to the state finals in tournament competition for a number of years, and won the state tournament on two occasions.

The basketball program came to be the focal point of the community's social life. Folks in the Hocking Hills of southern Ohio still speak of the glory years of their high school's basketball team.

The positive aspects of such a program are obvious. The program generated enthusiasm. It fostered in many youngsters the desire to live clean and healthy lives, stimulating many to work harder at academic achievement so that they would be eligible for athletic participation. It is difficult to find fault with these social and educational outcomes.

Some Cautions

Although the hard-sell has positive aspects, young coaches who are thinking of employing this form of program promotion should do so with extreme caution.

First, coaches should realize that conducting a broad-scale hard-sell sports program demands an enormous amount of their time and energy. In the case of the basketball coach described in the last section, family summer vacations had to be planned around the dates when boys aged eight through 18 attended the various workouts and participated in the scheduled summer leagues designed to develop basketball skills. And this is typical. Coaches employing heavy promotional tactics should be prepared to forego summer absences from their communities in the interest of overseeing developmental workouts. In fact, availability to organize summer sports programs becomes, in some communities, a barometer of a coach's enthusiasm.

Second, coaches should realize that, as a program mushrooms in size and scope, the expectations of the community become greater. The energy level of the coach must be sustained at a high level for long periods in order to accommodate the growing appetites of the "barnacles" who attach themselves to the program and who make the program the focal point of their own lives and fantasies.

Third, before excessive program expansion takes place, coaches should take note that growth is hard to reverse. Developing a program through hard-sell promotion is like walking a tightrope. Once one has started, it is far more difficult to turn back than to go on. Once peoples' imaginations have been triggered, their expectations dictate a pressure to expand the program, to discover ways to make it "even better." If, for example, coaches use a monthly or bi-annual newsletter as a vehicle of promotion, they must be prepared to sustain its publication regardless of growing costs in money, time, and energy. A coach's early commitment, therefore, to such a venture could later forestall the attainment of other goals to which the coach aspires.

Fourth, coaches would be well advised, especially in high visibility promotion, to keep administrators abreast of every planned development in program expansion and to insure administrative support of what they are doing. Administrators don't like surprises. But, when included in planning, they can become ardent allies to sports programs.

Last, human nature is such that those parents or fans who acquire power or status — and some do in the development of expansive high-visibility programs — frequently demand greater power. Many coaches have found that, if they are not cautious, they can become servants of support to promotional groups of their own creation. Administrators also must be alert to the course of hard-sell programs and the ambitions of coaches and boosters, lest they find themselves caught in compromising positions. A number of college athletic programs in recent years have suffered scandal because inattentive administrators have allowed insidious intrusions into program planning by interest groups with the wrong interests. One need not look far these days to see coaches, and even university presidents, suffering embarrassment from such intrusions. Indeed, some university presidents are no longer able to steer their educational ships without first considering the concerns of monied interests entangled in the athletic pursuits of their universities. At Southern Methodist University, the Governor of Texas, no less, was implicated in illegal payments to football players in a program gone amuck and later dealt the "death penalty" by the NCAA.

The "No hype" Approach

I have heard of a high school soccer coach in Vermont who so strongly dislikes promotion of any variety that he even refuses to post notices about the time and place of the first team meeting. His position is that those students interested in soccer will seek him out or learn of the program from past participants. He forbids parents or others to attend practice sessions saying, "I cannot conduct my classes in a theater atmosphere." Even post-season awards are taboo. Apparently, he wants students to learn that playing the game is sufficient reward and that further motivators only detract from the true value of the experience. When the season is over the coach encourages his players to participate in other sports, explaining that in this way they can broaden their interests and develop skills in activities that will serve them better later on in their lives.

This coach's teams have never experienced a losing season, and the interest level for his soccer program is greater than for any other sports program at the school. It would be difficult also to fault his practices on educational grounds.

A high school wrestling coach in Iowa took the low key approach to athletic coaching one step further. To ensure that the wrestlers on his team did not practice during the off season, this coach stored the mats and encouraged the members of his squad to discover other academic or athletic outlets that would enhance their overall growth. He even arranged student excursions into the city of Ames in order to "more fully acquaint them with the cultural amenities" of life. His home is a haven for student "rap" sessions and few faculty at the high school spend more time during the summer months leading students in community projects such as building park benches and helping the elderly. Interestingly, his wrestling teams have been at or near the top in league competitions for all his coaching years.

But coaches who adopt this coaching pattern must be conscious that others may well misinterpret the soft-sell as a sign of indifference. At least as many programs have floundered with the soft-sell approach as with the hard-sell.

✳ ✳ ✳ ✳ ✳

Obviously, there is room for many different kinds of sports programs in our schools. Indeed, variety is needed. Having both high visibility teams and low visibility teams can offer much to the varied likes of students. What is of greatest import is that coaches ascertain that the promotional approach they take fits their personalities and philosophies. A program's success is built on the fragile base of a coach's personality and his or her ability to use that personality in support of the desired promotional plan. More simply, the assessment of promotional direction is an important coaching decision and one that needs to be determined as early as possible in one's coaching adventure. It is not a decision that can be made by others, because only the coach can give the program it's direction, and because that direction must coincide with the coach's own manner of self-sell, goals and educational philosophy.

15
COMMUNICATION
for the health of the team

> Good, the more
> Communicated, more abundant grows.
> *On His Deceased Wife*, John Milton

"Flower, flower of the tower, what's the minute, what's the hour?", chortled the student pilot over the cockpit radio to the strict but lovable behemoth of a woman in the control tower at Bartow Air Base, a pilot training base near Cypress Gardens, Florida. The woman's sharp and immediate rejoinder: "Listen wise guy way up high, cease the crap or you won't fly."

This brief exchange that I overheard during my student-pilot military training is an example of communication — the simple act of exchanging thoughts.

Communication skills are especially vital to coaches because their work forces an almost non-stop experience of sharing themselves with others. The need to communicate makes itself evident in everything they do. Each day, in fact, coaches spend more time in communication than in any other endeavor.

The story is told of a man in an upstairs apartment who was preparing for bed. He took off one shoe and tossed it to the floor with a resounding thud. Recognizing that he had shattered the stillness of the evening, the man laid the other shoe down gently. This kept the lady in the apartment below awake most of the night, wondering when the other shoe would fall. Nobody likes to be left up in the air; we all yearn for a sense of completion. And good communication gives us that sense. When coaches try to communicate but fail, a sense of incompleteness seems to overcome them, sometimes gnawing at them in their sleep.

Breakdowns in Communication

A wife once said to her husband, "I know you believe you understand what you think I said, but I am not sure you realize that what you heard is not what I said." Lots of words, but little meaning getting through! Unfortunately, that is how attempts at communication often go.

The Ann Landers column, which appears in many newspapers, often includes letters from people seeking advice. One letter from a woman reader of the column contained a special request of Ms. Landers: "Please print your answer so my husband will read it." Imagine! Two people living in the same home, so unable to communicate that one calls on a newspaper columnist to say what she is unable to communicate directly to her own husband.

In athletics, similar examples of communication breakdowns are endless. Recently a young woman from our community returned from her freshman year in college. In her last year of high school she had broken all county and western-state scoring records in soccer as a striker for the high school team. She was recruited and labelled a "can't miss" player by several scouting services. In our conversation about her year at school, she spoke in glowing terms about her studies and friends, but she said this of her soccer experience: "I don't think I will play next year. My coach and I are not on the same wave length. I can't seem to express myself to her, and she won't express herself to me." Such failures of communication are unfortunate, for both players and coaches.

Followers of Oklahoma football fortunes became dispirited during the 1982-83 season when star fullback, Marcus Dupree, and head coach, Barry Switzer, seemed at odds over what Switzer called Dupree's "attitude and state of fitness." Dupree, who described himself as "laid-back," felt that he had only "so many" great runs in his body, and he wanted to save them for game situations. Switzer, sensing a nonchalance unbecoming a Sooner footballer, thought that Dupree's approach to the game lowered squad morale, violated tradition, and challenged "Sooner Spirit." Indeed, Switzer viewed Dupree as downright lazy. And Dupree felt Switzer to be unfairly intransigent. As this case so aptly portrays, if we wait until we feel like it or until all signals are go to communicate, we never will. But if we consciously set out to the task of communicating during hard times we will feel like it.

In this case, differences between a coach and a star player seemed more often discussed by local and national media than by the adversaries themselves. Assuredly, there would have been a better chance to resolve the deadlock of minds if the player and coach had forthrightly and directly discussed their concerns with each other. They never did, and the talented but disturbed Dupree left the program and school.

Of course not all communication problems are between players and coaches. Some of the worst communicative breakdowns occur within athletic departments where coaches are so enraptured by their own programs that schisms develop between colleagues. Indeed, I have seen departments in which petty animosities have mushroomed into departmental warfare, and lines of communications between coaches have been completely severed. In departments such as these even a modest sense of collegiality falls by the wayside. And, when this happens, the students are inevitably the losers.

Communicating without Words

In communicating with athletes, words are sometimes unnecessary. Communication can come from doing something rather than explaining it. The famous dancer, Pavlova, was once asked to interpret a very demanding dance she had just performed. Her response was, "Do you think I would have danced it if I could have said it?" Johann Goethe, the 18th century philosopher, supported Pavlova's thought when he said: "The highest cannot be spoken: it only can be acted."

"Bev" Jones, for many years an active platform speaker at summer student conferences, used to stress the importance of communication with the hands. Sometimes, the hands graphically reflect feelings, communicating soundlessly. The wringing of hands speaks to a sense of despair; the clapping of hands, joyousness; the folding of hands, reflective meditation or prayer. A smile, a frown, a smirk, a sneer, a shrug, a wink, a gesture — each indicates a sentiment. So these, too, are effective forms used in communication.

That verbal communication is important for a coach is beyond doubt, but other forms of communication are useful as well.

Sources of Problems

Problems frequently arise because coaches fail to communicate directly with players and even, at times, when it is obviously needed.

Once, in the middle of the football season, a coach told me about his plan to change quarterbacks for the upcoming Saturday game. The coach had talked with his assistants about the plan and had even discussed the change with the team captain and the sports information director. But by game day, he had still not talked about the plan with the regular quarterback, who had started every game for two seasons. Although the replaced quarterback had, by game day, heard rumors of the change, his first real knowledge of the fact came with the announcement of the starting line-ups. Only weeks later did the stunned, benched quarterback recover his confidence and again become a useful contributor to the team.

While players may disagree with coaching decisions like the one aforementioned, athletes may, at least, preserve respect for their coaches if decisions on matters as important as line-up changes are announced directly and tactfully to team members — and particularly to those immediately affected.

A second source of communication problems for coaches is the use of sarcasm and innuendo. When either is used, the person to whom the statement was directed must make an interpretive judgement. Was the coach joking or serious? Did the coach mean it? What was the message? Such questions commonly arise in response to sarcastic intonations. To avoid confusion or misunderstanding, coaches would be well served to shun sarcasm and derogatory intimations, especially when touching on subjects about which young athletes may be very sensitive.

A third problem is communication devoid of substance. While our interchanges of thoughts and opinions frequently do not go beyond the superficial level, coaches should be conscious that such exchanges rarely solve problems but that they hold the potential to create some.

A superficial exchange once transpired between a coach and an astronomer who found themselves sitting next to one another on a train. After they had identified their professions for one another, the astronomer said, "I'm not an athlete. My game is using my head!" Miffed at the inference that coaches do not use their minds, the coach replied, "My astronomy is Twinkle, Twinkle Little Star." What was gained here? Lacking substance, the exchange opened no doors and accomplished nothing but hurt feelings. Coaches should remember that the point of communication is to open doors, not to close them.

Inconsistency in communication is another source of problems for professional coaches. Players are ill at ease with coaches who are like chameleons in dealing with their athletes. When a coach greets with a smile on Wednesday and with a scowl on Thursday, that puts athletes on edge. Players can adjust to different styles, but they constantly want reinforcement on their state of acceptability with their coach — especially with a coach whose respect they seek. It is when coaches behavior is inconsistent or changes for no apparent reason that communication problems develop.

Responsibility for Good Communication

Far too many coaches I have known — some deeply respected for their tactical brilliance, charm, and persuasiveness in the recruitment of prospective student-athletes — are completely inept at communicating with the students in their charge. Perhaps this is because many coaches are pride-filled people who believe that what they have to offer is so valuable that young athletes must be ready either to "sacrifice" and "fall in line" with their dictates or "go packing."

I have heard coaches explain away player defections by saying that the players "just couldn't cut the mustard" or by using other cliches reflecting on players' lack of fortitude, loyalty, toughness, or intelligence. Sometimes the assessments are accurate. But far too often they reveal a breakdown in the coach's own inability to reach out, educate, and communicate.

I believe that, when problems arise, the major burden of responsibility in solving them lies with the coach, the adult. It is the coach who has been given the job of creating an atmosphere in which useful, open dialogue can take place. It befits his responsibility, then, to make the first effort to mend broken communication lines.

For college coaches, the responsibility may even be greater than for others, since the coach usually is instrumental in bringing the athlete to campus in the first place. The coach has accepted the athlete for better or worse and has made a commitment to care or share or do whatever else is necessary to make the union between the athlete, the coach, and the university a functional and productive one. None of this can take place if lines of verbal exchange between the parties are silent or severed.

Too often ignored in discussions of communication is that the word "communication" implies a communion—a sharing between two or more people. How frequently we find ourselves faulting an adversary for a lack of communication, forgetting that the fault must rest with more than one.

Coaches must keep their antennae ever skyward, extending always the first hand toward the reconciliation of any breakdowns.

Obviously, our awareness levels on matters of communication must be keen. The effectiveness of our work depends on it.

16
DISCIPLINE
drawing the boundary

> Where does discipline end? Where does cruelty begin? Somewhere between these, thousands of children inhabit a voiceless hell.
>
> Francois Mauriac

Many say that an inability to establish discipline in a team is the first indicator that the coach's career will be a short one. Indeed, athletic administrators hold discipline in such high regard that they frequently use it as the lone measuring-stick of a coach's effectiveness, especially when seeking a useful rationale for a coaching change. At the other end of the spectrum, however, are a few coaches who liken discipline to a brake on a drag racer, saying that concern with maintaining discipline only slows progress in more vital phases of their job. Most, I think, would agree that discipline in some form is essential and that, at the very least, it helps provide for athletes a refuge, a boundary, a guideline, even a sense of community. Athletes — especially young ones — function best in a setting where the expectations are understood and the rules are clear.

Too often, I fear, we think of discipline in athletics in terms of punishment and not in terms of its more frequent bearing — that of establishing a pattern of order in play and in personal growth through the play experience.

Discipline and Team Unity

Defined, discipline is a state of order maintained by training and control — a state requiring the regulation of conduct. It is an order that helps to establish habits that will serve a person in a productive way.

When students join a sport community, a team, they are in a sense consenting to an unwritten covenant. In biblical times, consent was marked through the sacrifice of an animal. In modern sports, consent is marked through the sacrifice of personal goals for the bigger interests of the team. Some coaches go so far as to erect signs like

THERE IS NO 'I' IN TEAM

to make their message clear to prospective combatants.

One cannot escape the immediacy of discipline in sports: discipline requires a response, not sometime, but now. Too many coaches pay little attention to this immediacy even in the conduct of their jobs and private lives. Listen to them:

When I make the salary I should, then you'll see team success.

Tomorrow, when I finish this pack of cigarettes, I'll start setting a better example.

Next week, when the season is over, I'll start spending more time with my family.

Eventually, I hope, my schedule will allow me to get involved with the players, but I simply can't at this time.

Many coaches labor under the delusion that "down the line" they will stumble onto the time they need to coach as they know they should. Of course, nothing could be further from the truth. Now or never is the acceptable time to commit one's coaching life to a disciplined style.

The process of creating discipline in a team involves developing a philosophical, or at least a procedural, uniformity—a behaving, reacting, or "marching" in order. The military creates this order physically through marching and other precision drills. In coaching, one attempts to discipline with total immersion. This involves the molding of the physical, emotional, even spiritual by making a team into a unity with a common line of thought, common behavior, and common goals.

K. C. Jones, the soft-spoken former coach of the successful Boston Celtics, has linked discipline to team camaraderie. The trademark of the Celtics has been their ability to prevent personal grievances from upsetting the feeling of respect for one another that has been essential to their winning tradition. "The main goal is to have player-to-player respect," Jones has said. "On a team with twelve players, you're not going to have everybody liking everybody." Jones has suggested that replacing dislike with an understanding respect is vital to his team's accomplishments. "If you have dislike," said Jones, "that reduces the team from 12 to 11, from 11 to ten, and right on down the line." Small wonder that Celtic coaches are usually former Celtic players with an understanding of the "liking" formula.

Establishing Discipline

Establishing discipline within a team requires salesmanship. Coaches must sell themselves and their team goals with sound explanations of the rationales behind dictums. They must win their teams' confidence and gain respect for their goals. If a team has a firm understanding of the necessity for the rules the coach has decreed, the team will usually follow the rules positively.

For students experiencing a first exposure to the ways of organized sports and the associated modes of discipline, a natural unsettling will develop. At this point, increased communication is valuable. But most athletes come to understand that some sacrifice of time, attitudes, and habits must be made in the disciplined life of the competitor. Some even seek out disciplinary guidelines when none are put forward by their mentors.

One of the early problems facing young coaches is in not knowing where to draw the line in establishing orders of discipline. Rules must be enforceable, and they should pertain directly to team performance or conduct. Random rule-making of the nit-picking variety too easily places coaches into the unwanted roles of police persons.

Many coaches have discovered that the most difficult aspect of students' personalities to bring to discipline is the emotional dimension. Anger and temper are natural emotions that are likely to appear spontaneously and suddenly. Coaches can be confident that their efforts in establishing a state of discipline have not been in vain when a hot-tempered teenager, slapped on the helmet by an opposing lineman, does not retaliate and incur a costly penalty but instead goes about his duties in a state of emotional control.

Lapses in Discipline

Large numbers of professional coaches have divorced themselves from any responsibility in matters of discipline to the point where embarrassment from bad publicity has befallen their teams. For example, an account in the "Etcetera" column of the *Athletic Director and Coach* several years ago cited a ruling by Northwest Orient Airlines that they would no longer transport members of the Chicago Bears, Green Bay Packers, or Detroit Lions because of ill-conduct on some flights. Even professional athletes should be expected to maintain a level of off-the-field conduct that would not necessitate such harsh action by a commercial carrier. Obviously the level of discipline of the athletes banned by Northwest Orient was extremely low.

When expectations regarding conduct are not met, the breakdown must be addressed if discipline is to be maintained; a coach can be assured of repeated transgressions if mistakes are only "wished away."

Calculated emotional tirades by coaches addressing their legions can occasionally be effective in accenting a code of discipline, but they lose their impact when overdone or over dramatized. Also, the overuse of the word "No" must be avoided. The occasional interjection of "Yes" lends credibility to disciplinary measures.

Foremost, when behavioral irregularities occur, a coach's response must be fair. If the coach is a fair person, respect will be won, and a disciplined team will be the product of the coach's objectivity.

Self-discipline

As a person who has coached team sports, I have come to understand the nuances of team discipline. What I have been less able to understand, but totally admire, are those individual athletes who, often without someone to direct them, discipline themselves.

One marathoner acquaintance has likened the experience of self-discipline to the action of the sun. She said,

> I don't have to see the sun to know light. In fact, by looking at the sun, I cannot see the accomplishments of sunlight for the blindness it causes. That which is around me — growing, emerging, living — is testimony to the sun's power. Indeed, it is seeing life that gives me strength during a long run. The beauty of that power regulates my daily regimen.

I suspect that such unlikely sources of inspiration, difficult for many of us to comprehend, motivate many early morning joggers to disciplined life-styles.

Imagine the discipline in the life of Penny Dean, the diminutive women's swim coach at the Pomona-Pitzer Colleges, who for years regimented her life around a pre-dawn rising followed by several hours of work at a ninety stroke per minute pace. In the afternoons, Dean took to the ocean for an additional four or five hours of rough sea-swimming, and she then went back to lap work in the pool for several hours. The payoff was the world record for the English Channel swim, which she bested by over an hour in 1978 and still holds today.

Those who saw the film The Karate Kid (I) had to marvel at the discipline at work in the martial art of Karate. Even more impressive to me were the revelations of a stroll through the Peoples' Park in Shanghai, China, at five in the morning. There, by the thousands, and of their own volition, people were performing the daily ritual of Tai Chi, a discipline in the coordination of mind and body.

John Eusden, in his book *Zen and Christian*, has written of the discipline accompanying the art of Aikido: "The student is urged to join the cosmic energy flow and to mold her particular activity with it." To discover this "life energy" or *ki* is to move away from ego and develop "no mind" about one's self and activities.

Approaches to Discipline

Quite naturally, points of emphasis concerning discipline will vary from one coach to another.

Some feel that the personal, off-the-court conduct of players requires regulation. One such coach is Eddie Robinson, the winningest college football coach ever, whose regimen of discipline includes his personal presence at the team's early morning risings. "I get to the dorm at 6:15 every morning and ring a bell," Robinson explains. "If [the athletes] stay in bed, I'll ring the bell in their ear, and the only way they can get me to stop is if their feet hit the floor." Robinson goes on: "I don't make them go to class, but I do make them go to breakfast. I figure if they get that far, they'll go on to class. It may be crude, but it works."

Other coaches reject Robinson's concern with off-the-court rules of behavior and focus instead on discipline in the pool or playing field. One opponent of the Robinson approach has, in fact, said, "I don't give a hoot about what [the athletes] eat or where they sleep. They become my babies when they hit the floor."

We might easily take issue with either position, but not with the general recognition that, in the building of teams, discipline of some form is necessary. It simply reflects on the fact that the coach cares.

Robert Redford, the fine actor, has spoken of another, harsher form of discipline in explaining why his own football interests were short-lived. Said Redford,

> I got tired of the one-dimensional life of the athlete. It was just a constant, tiresome round of practice and steaks. I never knew what it was like just to enjoy a sport. I was always out there groveling to win. You begin to fear not winning. One day I realized how narrow my life had been, that I disliked the system that produces test tube athletes.

Discipline, though necessary, need not be that confining.

Bill Manlove, the respected football coach of Widener College, has offered what he calls the TWIGS approach to discipline. His feelings reflect the importance of teams doing things together. "Only with a discipline that fosters togetherness can success be realized," says Manlove. In explaining his concept of discipline, Manlove talks about the twigs on a tree's branch. While a single twig is easily broken, put a group of twigs together and they become as strong as the branch itself. Thus Manlove uses the letters "TWIGS" to abbreviate the phrase "Together We Inherit Great Strength."

One junior high school coach I know devised a pattern of living formula for his teams in order to develop an understanding of discipline. He established a system of "buddies," a pairing of students, with one serving as a designated leader for a week. During the late summer practices, buddies would spend their days together. If the leader wanted to walk to town, they both walked to town, the follower acceding to the leader's desires. It was not the follower's place to question why, only to respond to the will of the leader. The coach found a measure of success in this formula.

Saying No

The first coach I ever came to know well was a man of grand humor but stern rule who coached my high school baseball team. Each year, Howard Ferguson would ceremoniously close the classroom door at the first team meeting of the Spring promptly at 3:00. Then he would in emphatic tones say to the candidates for the baseball team, "NO is a word you will hear a lot. Come to love it, because it will save you." Those who attempted to enter the room after 3:00 were loudly told that they were no longer candidates. That our baseball lives would be governed by rules was never left in doubt.

In a permissive society, like that in present-day America, the word "No" is not often heard. But young people need to hear it — not necessarily spoken harshly, but as a guide to what counts as approved behavior. In sports, athletes sometimes hear "No" in a different context. The star quarterback of his high school arrives on the college campus and is told, "No, you will not be our #1 quarterback on the first day of practice; on the depth chart you will be the #8 quarterback and #2 cornerback." There is a message here. Can the athlete discipline his ego, relinquish his dreams of quarterbacking grandeur, and accept the role of a second string "meatman" because that is where he is needed? Perhaps, but this is often the introduction to sport discipline — sometimes intentionally used as a test of an athletes' ability to adapt or to take orders.

※ ※ ※ ※ ※

The best sports discipline is that which makes the athlete a better athlete and the coach a better coach. Both athlete and coach can become more productive people through experiences in sports in which a standard of discipline provides team direction.

102 OFF THE BENCH

17
SPORTSMANSHIP
a coaching priority?

> For when the One Great Scorer comes
> To write against your name,
> He marks — not that you won or lost —
> But how you played the game.
> Grantland Rice

Basic to the coaching profession is the belief that, of equal importance to the goals we set for our teams, are the methods we use to achieve those goals. The standards by which we live as coaches and athletes must be as high as the achievements we seek.

Current Attitudes

"Whatever happened to sportsmanship, fair play?", wrote Jim Murray in the *Los Angeles Times* following the destructive activities of Detroit Tiger fans, triggered perhaps by actions of players on the field, in the aftermath of the 1984 World Series.

Our society, it seems, has lost some of its regard for the purity of sports epitomized in good sportsmanship. A few sociologists have rested the blame on the drug culture, on high salaries in professional sports, and even on subconscious attitudes resulting from the ignominies of the Vietnam War.

I vividly recall hearing about one incident of unsportsmanlike behavior while seated at the speakers' table in the gymnasium-turned-banquet-hall of an Ohio high school, waiting to address the gathered athletes and parents on the subject of sportsmanship. Apparently, in the hectic last seconds of an eighth grade basketball game, the home team trailed by one point and had no time-outs left. The home team's coach screamed to one of his players

"Joey, you're hurt!" and the player "smartly" responded by falling to the floor, feigning injury, and causing the referees to call an officials' time-out. This act of "quick thinking" allowed a new player to be inserted into the game with instructions from the bench for a designed last shot. The home team set up the shot and indeed won the game — none of which would have happened without the time-out.

What was most alarming to me was that each adult at the table with me reflected on the occurrence with favor — one even suggesting that the alert, "quick thinking" coach be considered for promotion to the varsity staff!

Several months before, I had been officiating a AYSO soccer game — the Blue Shirts against the Red Shirts. In the late stages of the game, following three consecutive missed headers by a peewee halfback on the Red Shirt team, the Red Shirt coach pulled the embarrassed youngster from the game, loudly chastising him for being a "chicken." As though this coach's despicable act was not enough, the Blue Shirt coach, in his half-time talk, urged his players to ridicule the Red Shirt players with chants of "Chicken, chicken, yellow chicken" during the course of play in the second half.

Other sports, too, have their improprieties: The slow trot around the bases after a home run, the taunting dance of defensive linemen over a fallen quarterback, and the intimidating antics of hockey players. Yet, almost every weekend, readily visible on television and in stadia and arenas around the country, similar episodes or worse are carried out by collegians and professional athletes for young eyes to observe. Little wonder, then, that many view as *acceptable* incidents like those I have described happening in children's leagues. But, if such actions are acceptable nowadays, it is time for coaches to take a long look at the kind of leadership in sportsmanship they are providing.

How much more sporting it would be to steer budding athletes toward attitudes of respect for actions like those of Mats Wilander, the Swedish tennis star. On the way to the French Open Championships in 1983, in a match with Jose Luis Clerc, Wilander refused a questionable call on match point that would have made him the winner. "I cannot win this way," said Wilander, and he ordered the point replayed.

Negativism

In many locker rooms, it has become "chic" to indulge in excuse-making, a form of unsportsmanlike behavior that detracts from an opponent's accomplishments. Last year, for example, a professional basketball coach cited "torrid temperatures in the arena" and "liberal officiating which favored the physical play of the opponents" as reasons for his team's loss. But it is easier to find fault after a game than to solve a problem before or during one.

Many coaches feel smug and self-satisfied if they simply point out other people's faults. But this is negative, and living on negatives is self-defeating, counter-productive, and detrimental to the teaching of sportsmanship.

Part of the difficulty rests in the failure to understand that excuse making or denigration of opponents detracts from the accomplishments of the foe and is therefore unsportsmanlike.

Clarence Chaffee, legendary coach of the Williams College soccer and tennis teams and a national Super Seniors (80 or older) tennis champion, once lectured my women's team at Williams on the subject of sportsmanship. As "Chafe" pointed out, no word or deed used to gain an unfair advantage has a place on the court of play. He further explained that, because unsportsmanlike acts are almost always used to give the user an (often unearned) advantage or sense of superiority, they are almost always negative.

I am reminded of the story of a small town volunteer fire department chief who was asked what his firemen did first when called to a fire. "We drench the entire area with water, knock out the windows, and chop up the furniture," he replied. "What next?" he was asked. "The second thing we do," replied the Chief, "is to make absolutely sure we're at the right address."

While this is only a story, it does point to the sad human tendency to get into the demolition business. We do a good job of tearing down, but not so good a job of building up. We are more ready to be negative, to take advantage, than to be positive and fair. The educator-coach must not participate in such negativism but must work hard, through sports, to correct it.

There is a growing pattern that suggests that, if we have been wronged, we must get even and teach our opponents the lessons they deserve. Projected into the world's arenas, this attitude supports the philosophy that violence must be answered with violence. The people of South Africa, Lebanon, Colombia, and Ireland — to name just a few countries — are learning that this philosophy of requital does not work.

The Coach's Responsibility

As coaches, we can do much to correct attitudes relating to sportsmanship. We can best do this, it seems to me, by carrying out our special responsibilities for restraint and civility and by affirming the rights of other coaches, parents, fans, and players who hold attitudes and goals different from our own. Certainly despair is not the answer. Coaches must not ignore ignoble acts by athletes, writing them off as "signs of the times" or justifying inaction with other excuses.

A few years ago, my wife accidentally scratched a piece of antique furniture that she especially liked, and she felt badly about it. When she told an elderly New Hampshire friend about it, she was advised, "Rub the scratches with oil and they will disappear." The remedy for unsportsmanlike behavior may not be as easy as the one for scratches on antique furniture, because the hurt has impacted other people, but developing favorable sportsmanlike behavior patterns is, in fact, possible.

When I was a young boy, I relished hearing the weekly radio episodes of the Lone Ranger. "Return with us now to those thrilling days of yesteryear...The Lone Ranger," intoned the narrator. And then I thrilled, like thousands of others who turned the pages of history, to the great deeds of this "champion of justice who fought for law and order in the early Western United States." Young listeners of that era became attuned to the priorities of fair play, to the rights of underlings, and to justice. Certainly coaches have the opportunity to be modern day Lone Rangers as well as tacticians.

An ancient Chinese proverb reads, "It is better to light a candle than to curse the darkness." What has happened and continues to happen in the conduct of sports is cause for curse, but coaches will be better served, as will our society, if they carry the torch of good sportsmanship and pass it freely to the young athletes who follow their lead. Sportsmanship is not dead; it needs only to be re-emphasized. Coaches must reach out to athletes, setting examples with their own actions. They must always remember that, in the final analysis, how the game is played and not the game's final outcome is what truly matters.

18
CREATING A MORAL SENSE
a use for a coach's influence

> A man is truly ethical only when he obeys the compulsion to help all life which he is able to assist, and shrinks from injuring anything that lives.
>
> *The Philosophy of Civilization*, Albert Schweitzer

I have heard coaches suggest that moral leadership on their part is not a facet of their job — that parents have total responsibility for their children's moral development. I have also heard it suggested that to help athletes make moral judgements is to intrude into matters better left to priests, rabbis, pastors, or other professional clergy.

Parents and clergy do of course have major responsibilities for the rearing of children. But a great deal of obligation also falls on the "extended family" of adult coaches whose work directly touches young people. Coaches probably have more impact on young minds, in fact, than any other group of professionals in our society, and they can therefore help athletes with sound moral counsel.

Coaches as Educators

Coaches are educated people who wield greater power and take on wider responsibility than many in academe because of their training in people orientation.

Dr. Robert Oppenheimer, a scientist who was one of the planners of the atomic bomb and knew of its potentially destructive powers, requested that the first bomb be dropped, not on Hiroshima, but on an uninhabited island off the Japanese coast. Unfortunately his request was rejected. It is ironic that education, acclaimed as vital to our survival, can also provide the type of knowledge that can be tragically misused. Education must always be accompanied by moral responsibility — and coaches are, first and foremost, educators.

A philosopher friend once told of the great cellist Pablo Casals who made a similar point about artists. Besides being one of the finest musicians of the twentieth century, Casals was a man with deep convictions about rules of conduct. Casals once wrote,

> I know that there are those who believe that an artist should live in an ivory tower, removed from the struggles and suffering of their fellow men. That is a concept to which I have never been able to subscribe. An affront to human dignity is an affront to me; and to protest injustice is a matter of conscience. Are human rights of less importance to an artist than to other men? Does being an artist exempt one from his obligations as a man? If anything, the artist has a particular responsibility because his voice may be heard when other voices are not.

Casals and Oppenheimer were right. People in the position to inspire have special responsibilities to speak out and act. And, like artists and scientists, coaches are positioned to inspire. Indeed, working with a subject (sports) that students love, coaches have the attention of young people to a greater degree than most others who impact youth. Coaches must therefore respond to the call by dealing with moral issues directly.

I understand the temptations facing coaches to put potentially confrontational moral or ethical issues on the laps of parents or other professionals. It certainly is far simpler to lay such issues aside than to address them directly. But, by pretending that a situation involving theft of a stereo by one team member from another would work itself out, one college basketball coach watched a season disintegrate into feelings of distrust and bitterness. That kind of evasion of moral responsibility is dishonest. Dishonesty in athletic practices will not drive out dishonesty. Only a moral sense will do that.

At least for those coaches who hold educational positions in schools, colleges, and universities, responsibility for teaching about moral and ethical matters is inescapable. This is not an easy responsibility to bear because it demands that coaches, if they are to retain any credibility with their students, must attempt to direct lives toward goodness and try, at least, to live exemplary lives.

CREATING A MORAL SENSE 109

Society's Stance on Morality

Many who followed the events of the Pan American Games in Caracas, Venezuela, in 1983 were shaken by the stories of "drug" scandal. On one account, an American weight lifter was stripped of three gold medals because he was found to have used anabolic steroids to build strength. Thirteen other American athletes left Caracas abruptly, obviously to avoid drug testing. Our country stood embarrassed before the eyes of the world. Little wonder that many young athletes take the practice of "cheating the system" to be a part of the game.

Harold Enarson, President Emeritus of Ohio State University, in a 1985 speech to the Association of Governing Boards of State Universities, deplored the moral chaos he saw in the lives of young people and zeroed in on some of the violations of moral integrity facing modern sports. Said Enarson:

> All signals are flashing red when student-athletes are admitted in violation of...admission requirements, when the evaluation of academic transcripts is subverted, when grades are falsified..., when there are phantom classes and forged transcripts, when blue-chip athletes are recruited and routed to junior colleges to gain minimum eligibility.

Enarson went on to point out that governors, legislators, and business leaders sometimes also support unethical practices by entertaining prospective athletes and promising them future employment.

Then is the world for future generations in chaos, as is often asserted? In a paper "A New Look at the Prophets" by David Held, the famed journalist Dorothy Thompson is quoted as suggesting that the world's dilemmas rest on the moral break-downs of mankind.

> In the many years during which I have been living and admiring it, this planet has never failed to turn on its axis with exact mathematical certitude; the sun has never failed to rise and set; Arcturus has always appeared in exactly the same relationship to the constellation of the Bear...an acorn has always produced an oak and not an elm...and the wild ducks always wheel southward at the same time...No, the world is not in chaos. Men are in chaos.

There is truth here. The world hasn't jumped the track, but people — including many coaches and others associated with sports — have.

Education, Technology, and Morality

Most would agree that ignorance and illiteracy are impediments to the good life: education offers understanding and power. But understanding and power may be put either to fruitful or to evil use. The educated criminal is considerably more dangerous than the uneducated. Though vital to us, education is not the entire answer to our moral problems.

Nor is technology. The same chemistry that has produced healing drugs has also created addictive drugs, which pose chronic problems for many athletic programs. The same nuclear power that awakens new hope can also inflict catastrophe. A sense of ethics must accompany technological progress if the products of our labors are truly to benefit mankind.

The New York World's Fair of 1964 contained many exhibits about technology. One traced the history of human communication from early cave drawings to today's space technology. Another depicted ways human beings have used energy through the centuries and prospects for its future use. Yet another illustrated the evolution of transportation from the invention of the wheel to satellite shuttles of the future. When viewing exhibits like these, one cannot help but reflect on the progress of humanity.

Unfortunately, though, our progress does not show signs of moral maturity. Most indicators point to the fact that modern technology has far outdistanced modern morality. Not only can we live more easily and travel faster, but we can also exploit people more effectively, neglect them willfully, and kill them more efficiently.

While education and technology may serve us, we should realize that they must be accompanied by a sense of ethics if they are truly to benefit humankind. If we disregard morality, we ultimately suffer the consequences. Of course, not all human tragedy can be blamed on immorality. But there are basic moral truths, and the result of ignoring them is always calamity.

The Social Context

The coach's job has been made more difficult by the transgressions of our society. The ethical ideals that educated societies have traditionally held dear have eroded, and evidence of the erosion abounds in the coach's daily work with student-athletes.

I recently watched in disbelief as a visiting college coach, seated with athletes at a training meal, roared in supportive laughter as his athletes conducted a food throwing party that disrupted the mealtime for hundreds of students and left the dining hall in a state of utter disarray. The coach's attitude mirrored our society's acceptance of political, economic, social, and ecological ills.

We Americans possess a disproportionate share of the world's telephones, automobiles, and other luxuries and are quite used to using the earth's natural resources at a rate exceeding the earth's carrying capacity. Much of the damage we are perpetrating is irreversible. America, thought to be one of the most cultured and technologically advanced of the world's nations, continues its gradual destruction of the quality of life for future generations by reducing the ability of our forests and waterways to make oxygen, polluting the immediate atmosphere, destroying the ozone layer above, and thus poisoning the air we breathe. Damage to soil and water will surely affect man's ability to satisfy the world's food needs. On top of that, Americans waste more than one quarter of our own food supplies. That, too, is immoral.

Dr. Norman Cousins, in his book *The Healing Heart: Antidotes to Pain and Helplessness*, has pointed out that immoralities stretch even to the world of sports in society's approval of the "legal brain battering" euphemistically called prizefighting. As Cousins says, the human brain is "the most exquisitely fashioned, fragile, and complex mechanism in the universe." Yet in boxing the human fist "can produce enough force to damage the tender tissue inside the shell." Cousins questions the conscience of a society that gains pleasure "from witnessing these legalized assaults perpetrated by the participants until one is battered into unconsciousness, generally the result of burst blood vessels inside the brain."

Clearly, if coaches are to have an impact within a society of such extravagance and violence, they need to isolate those examples in their coach/team experiences that will raise athletes' levels of consciousness about their moral responsibilities.

Coaches influence the minds that, down the road, will set the patterns and lay down rules for survival. If coaches tolerate disdain for other's property or well being in their own lives, if they condone wastefulness at training tables or "stops at McDonald's," if they turn their backs to sexual promiscuity knowing that it is infringing on other's lives, if they make light of overindulgence, then they are not being proper caretakers of the precious lives in their trust and care.

As a coaching comrade suggested at a Fellowship of Christian Athlete's Coaches' Conference in Silver Bay, New York, "The greatest service a coach can render to a student-athlete is to teach that person how to succeed. This can only be accomplished when a deep respect for other's thoughts, behaviorisms, and lives is created."

This coach went on to speak of an incident, involving himself as a high school athlete, which provides an example of how coaches can effect the moral judgements made by young people:

> I was walking along the beach one day with two of my buddies. We were wearing matching tee-shirts on which were imprinted in bold letters the words "HELP STAMP OUT VIRGINITY." Fatefully, we happened upon our football coach and his wife and daughter who were also walking on the beach. After greeting us, the coach looked hard at our shirts, unsmiling. Then, quite suddenly, Coach spun around and angrily ordered us to take the shirts off. We did so with no question. He then ordered us to take them home, wash them, fold them up, and put them into boxes. Then he said, 'I want you to store them until that magical day when your daughters are preparing for their first dates — then give the box with its contents to the boys who come to take them out.' The impact was immediate. So moved was I by that encounter, that my entire attitude toward sexual morality was changed forever. My respect for that coach has no bounds. I thank him for his caring.

Unfortunately, in this litigious age, it seems that few coaches risk such intrusions into other people's "rights."

New Developments

Hopeful signs have, in fact, begun to emerge. At the so-called "integrity convention" of the NCAA in New Orleans in 1985, proposals to curb cheating in athletics were passed for immediate implementation.

In his kickoff address at those meetings, then President John Ryan of Indiana University summoned all presidents, directors, and coaches to join in the march for reform. "Presidents are heartsick" he said, "at the integrity crisis in athletics."

Those of us who attended that special session then voted overwhelmingly to support a dozen proposals on such issues as athletic self-study programs, academic reporting (of entrance requirements, high school GPA, test scores, eligibility requirements, and graduation rates), penalties for repeated violations of NCAA regulations, coaches' penalties for violations, student-athletes' accountability, budget control, audits, length of playing seasons, numbers of contests, compliance affidavits, and playing rules. If the entire coaching profession would adhere to these proposals in the spirit of fair play, the future in college athletics would be ethically brighter.

※ ※ ※ ※ ※

Being a coach is not a no-win occupation. For the most part, the students with whom coaches work turn out far better than the coaches have any right to expect. But coaches need constantly to remind themselves that their students are loaned treasures who belong to this world and must serve it after they leave the tutelage of their coaches. It is therefore important that coaches do their part in turning youth over to the world as better people than when they were entrusted to them.

Seen in this light, the profession of coaching carries great responsibilities with it. And, to these responsibilities, coaches are morally bound.

19
EMOTION
a question of how much

> When you walk in love
> With the wind on your wing
> And cover the earth
> With the song you sing
> The miles fly by.
> "Joy is like the Rain", Sister Miriam Therese

Because of the intensely competitive nature of collegiate athletics, coaches often stimulate emotional peaks in athletes in an attempt to better performances. Anyone who has coached for any length of time has called for emotional expression in the course of an athletic contest or in preparation for one.

Natural Responses

In discussions with basketball coaches on the topic of striving for emotional response as a coaching tool, I have heard various opinions. On one side of the issue are coaches who insist that athletes should be taught to suppress emotions, to play the game in a "businesslike way" or on the "intellectual level" only. On the other side are those who, viewing emotion as at least one facet of what sports are all about, often endorse the use of adrenaline-charging pre-game pep talks that "hype" players to super feats. I have seen coaches employing both approaches lead teams that have performed admirably.

My own coaching comfort zone called for allowing emotional responses to occur naturally. I found the natural release of emotion to be healthy, and it also relieved me of the sometimes onerous task of purposefully developing schemes to instill emotion or repress it. I think that accepting the spontaneous flow of emotion also allows the nature of the rivalry, the competitive situation, the crowd's excitement, and other intangibles to have their natural affect on teams. Most important, I've found, it removes the likelihood of emotional extremes entering the fray, helps perspective, and allows room for emotional recovery after contests have concluded.

But clearly there is no right or wrong practice for administering emotional control. Nor is there any consensus on whether coaches should "play emotional games" with their players. At least one psychologist has recommended that, before establishing hard-and-fast rules regarding emotional control, coaches should weigh those rules against their own team goals and against the personality or "chemistry" of the team. This seems to me to be good counsel.

John McEnroe, one of the world's finest tennis players, has long maintained that his emotional outbursts, despite the controversy they create, help his concentration and "charge his game." In stark contrast, the stoic, expressionless Bjorn Borg "disallowed" emotions to "interfere with his rhythm." Both are excellent performers.

Regardless of the attitudes a coach might hold on the level of emphasis that should be placed on emotion, it is extremely important that the coach recognize the aim of the educational endeavor: to teach young athletes to think and to make reasoned decisions. It is an educational mandate that in our teaching and coaching we encourage the thought process. In doing so, we will help to develop a maturity and self-confidence that will serve the members of our teams well in the long run. And, if coaches feel that thinking will not be thwarted by a free expression of emotion, they should not inhibit its natural flow.

Love

Most coaches would agree that the glue holding teams together — the magical, intangible ingredient that creates cohesion and team camaraderie — includes at least one emotion: love. I speak here, not of romantic love, but of the strong predilection of enduring loyalty to a person (such as a coach) or a group (such as a team).

Football Coach Jim Wacker of Texas Christian University, who gained notoriety for suspending six players (including Heisman Award candidate Kenneth Davis) for accepting illicit payments from boosters, has said, "My players need love. We all need love." Love is, in fact, what Wacker counted on to keep his team together in the wake of his dismissals. And those who followed the fortunes of the Villanova basketball team during their Cinderella season of 1985 must hold vivid memories of the love that the team claimed to be the "potion of their power."

Love has a way of challenging us to reach out to neighbors and to have compassion for our enemies. But in its full expression, love can be painful as well as beautiful.

Soon after the termination of America's involvement in the Vietnam War, I accompanied an eleven-year-old, orphaned, Vietnamese boy to Kennedy Airport. Like other "boat people," the boy had found a home in America, but he held little hope of seeing his family again and feared their demise. On a tip from the Red Cross that a particular flight to Kennedy would be bringing a small girl who might be the boy's sister, we drove to the airport. Might the boy's sister, like the boy himself, have miraculously survived when the ill-fated boat on which the family had sought freedom met peril in the South China Sea?

At the airport, the boy spotted his sister and the reunion was wordless. Each, standing for seemingly endless moments with tear-filled eyes, stared at the other. Then, like magnets, they came together. Quickly, they moved to a secluded corner of the terminal to share a gorgeous love with one another.

While coaches rarely encounter love of this intensity, some of my fondest memories of life as a coach are of moments when the spirit of love has surfaced — teammate for teammate, player for coach, or coach for player. In fact, the epitome of the competitive experience, I have found, is the full and honest expression of love that athletes develop for one another. We have all seen this love in the embraces of victors and losers, in the broad smiles, in joyful tears, the clasped hands, and hugging bodies following a hotly contested game.

Coaches can foster love in a variety of ways. They can forgive; they can defuse anger; they can relieve fear; and they can heal emotional hurts. Love builds friendships, forgiveness reconciles personal animosities, and sympathy prompts deeds of social righteousness. Perhaps we cannot alter human nature, but through love we can try to improve human relationships.

Even in professional sports, unselfish love based on mutual respect is not unusual. The highly publicized "Celtic Pride" is more than a couple of words on bumper stickers in the New England area. The words describe the love, first catalyzed by the renowned Red Auerbach and Bill Russell, that the team's members have traditionally felt for one another. And one need only to view a reunion of the "Pack," the burly men who made up Vince

Lombardi's Green Bay Packer teams, to understand the special place of love in their success story.

Coaches can discover love at any level. As coaches, we have the freedom to give our feelings of love to those with whom we live and work, to be honest with them, to care enough to tell them the truth, to share our talents and our time with them. We have received our lives without charge; we must give our lives without cost. Freely given, love is what makes team relationships strong and athletic experiences meaningful.

George Plimpton has described the group of physical misfits who made up the Baltimore Colts during their heyday in the National Football League. Led by a sunken-chested, knock-kneed quarterback named Johnny Unitas and an almost blind, slow-legged wide receiver named Raymond Berry, the Colts wound together so many fibers of inner strength that they were the best team in professional football for a number of years. In describing these Colts, Plimpton emphasizes that their caring for one another was the force that solidified the team.

The only time that love can work against team success is when it is qualified. The wife of a coach I know tells the story of how her husband once yelled angrily at children making footprints in the concrete he had just laid in a sidewalk. "I thought you loved children," she said. "I do," he replied, "but in the abstract, not in the concrete." Team love is greatest when not qualified in this, or any other, way.

Fear and Anger

Opposed to love are the less idyllic emotions of fear and anger.

Like love, these emotions can be very useful. Most of us learned in infancy to fear fire, for example. This learned emotional response can serve to protect us when we work near fire, and it alarms us when we hear or smell smoke. Fear has a way of bringing about a humbling respect for strength or power. Like a child avoiding a bully for fear of being "beat up," an athlete pushes the caution button when caution can be useful. And there is nothing wrong with that.

With nightmarish reality, I can still see the scene in the men's barracks of the World War II Japanese prisoner-of-war camp in the Philippine Islands following the escape of two men from the compound where I was an internee. Japanese soldiers stormed angrily into the barracks, bayonets drawn. Shouting, they force-searched all the prisoners. Their threats on our lives seemed terribly real. Only hindsight revealed that those threats were a show of force designed to strike fear into our hearts as a deterrent to any future plans for escape. The threats had a persuading effect.

Still, caution must be observed as to when and how fear is used as a coaching tool. The most dastardly labels coaches can use, I have found, are those that brand an athlete as fearful. I cringe at the flippant use of words like "chicken," "coward," or "choker" which are too commonly and frivolously used to describe athletes. Use of these terms in earshot of athletes almost insures a performance to fit the label, especially if the athletes are young. When athletes hear these words, their self-confidence is dashed and their self-esteem lowered, leaving them incapable of meeting the challenge of the moment.

Like fear, anger can be a useful emotion, but it must be used cautiously. There is a sense of calm, even relief, following the venting of pent up anger through verbal exhortation or physical action. But very few athletes perform at consistently high levels when angry. And only one person's feelings are soothed when a person directs vindictive anger toward another.

Although a few athletes do perform well in a state of anger, coaches should not leap to the conclusion that anger is the milieu we should strive to create for athletes when preparing for athletic contests. In fact, coaches would do well to recognize the destruction that can result when uncontrolled anger is unleashed in sports. The potential for injury or worse is especially great when the sight of athletes unleashing their angry emotions triggers a response in spectators. A mob's reaction to unharnessed anger may be uncontrollable fury that can result in property destruction, injury, or even death. Such fury in soccer stadia around the world has, in recent years, caused calamitous losses of human life.

Sometimes, a coach's expression of anger can be so negative that it has the potential of destroying an athlete's confidence forever. Once, when watching a Little League baseball game at Ellsworth Air Force Base in South Dakota, I saw a small second baseman make two consecutive errors. The boy's coach, who was also his father, and obviously embarrassed by his son's miscues, angrily marched out to the lad who was squatting on second base and hiding his face in his glove. The coach grabbed the boy, turned him so that his back faced the spectators, and loudly said, "Let the folks see your spine — it's yellow!" I doubt that the second baseman ever again enjoyed a game of baseball or, for that matter, any other athletic contest.

I am reminded also of an emotional episode involving the first high school baseball team I coached. It was a good team made better by the talents of a left-handed pitcher whose statistics attracted professional scouts to many of our games. Since we had tied a rival high school for the league championship, our team played the rival to determine which team would represent the league in the state tournament. Playing at our opponent's home field in the play-off game, we entered the bottom half of the ninth inning tied. With two outs, their top hitter looped a fly ball that bounced away from our right fielder for a triple. We intentionally walked the next two batters to create a force play at any base, and our young lefty immediately threw two strikes past the next batter. Then the most bizarre thing happened. As our pitcher began his windup for the next delivery, the opposing coach leaped into the air from his third base coaching box and shouted, "Balk! Balk!" Startled, the pitcher stopped his motion toward home plate and *was* immediately charged with a balk. The winning run walked across the plate as we all gaped in anguish and horror. More alarming, the next day the local paper quoted the winning coach as crediting his team's victory to our young pitcher's having "choked in the clutch"! Interestingly, this same coach, who scolded other coaches who had seen the game for being "poor sports" when the episode was brought up for discussion at a post-season league meeting, was later awarded "coach of the year" honors. The young left-hander, overcome by a fear of failure, lost some of his affection for the game and was never again as effective a pitcher as he had been.

Experienced coaches know that fear of contact, fear of failure, and fear of fear are common in athletes, especially in their developing years. But fears of these sorts usually are conquered if coaches counsel athletes in a *positive* manner.

Mixed Feelings

I have always held an aversion for things mixed. I become ill at ease when things around me are mixed up or unsettled. I particularly dislike mixed vegetables, mixed drinks, or mixed doubles. And, in my coaching life, I become suspect when players talk to me "with mixed feelings" — about a teammate, a coach, a style of play, or a desire to play more. My initial response is usually, "Let's unmix those feelings."

I can think of few mixed emotions or feelings that serve a team well. Envy, jealousy, frustration, anxiety, hatred — mixed emotions all — rarely lead to anything positive. In sports, such emotions serve only to erode, undermine, or destroy programs. Any coach seeking to realize the full potential of a group of athletes should realize that these feelings work insidiously on the minds of players, toughening the coaching task considerably.

The most difficult job in dealing with mixed feelings is to identify the real problem. Only then can the "unmixing" take place so that the problem can be addressed. When this doesn't happen, a player may quit a team, another casualty of unresolved mixed emotions. Coaches are often satisfied with this solution because it is the easiest resolution to a sticky problem and because it relieves a nagging tension. The easiest resolution, however, is not necessarily the best. It is imperative for coaches to make diligent efforts to help young athletes come to grips with such perplexing feelings.

One mixed emotion — hatred — is a sickness with a particularly eroding effect on human personalities since it has a way of destroying objective thought. I recall with gratitude my mother's valiant efforts to erase hatred from the minds of her children during our years as prisoners of war under the Japanese. When most conversations among prisoners centered on "Hate Jap" stories, Mom forbade our even whispering such bigoted sentiments and included the Japanese garrison as benefactors of love in her nightly prayers. Only with such guidance could I manage, forty years later, to accept an invitation from Rokuro Tomibe, our prison commandant, to be a guest in his home in Kyoto.

Coaches must make every effort to rid themselves of hate-filled emotions. Objectivity and, therefore, competence as professional leaders of impressionable young minds will be lost if they do not.

Clearly, emotions impact athletic performances to such an extent that it is important for coaches to ponder seriously how they can better direct emotional tides to best serve students, psychologically and educationally.

20
SUBSTANCE ABUSE
a no-win remedy in Sport

Drink has drained more blood,
Plunged more people into bankruptcy,
Slain more children,
Dethroned more reason,...
Driven more to suicide, and
Dug more graves than any other poisoned scourge that ever swept
the death-dashing waves across the world.

Evangeline Cory Booth

Bees make hives, beavers build dams, birds weave nests, and moles burrow holes. But what these animals do is no different from what other animals have done for centuries; they repeat patterns of creation rather than initiate new ones. Humans, however, are an innovative species — especially in sports. Aided by science, the sports world has made continuous progress in the development of techniques and training methods. Sports medicine has developed fantastic methods for quickening recuperation. Dietary research has given coaches a better basis for judging which eating patterns help performance. And studies on human motion have made giant strides in answering questions about the best ways to condition the human body as well as the best ways to dive, jump, run, kick, and throw.

The depressing news is that, in our haste to achieve greater speeds, lift greater weights, and throw longer and harder, we have often taken routes that promise shortcuts. Substance abuse is one such route.

Former Chief Justice Earl Warren, in explaining why he always turned to the sports pages of the newspaper first, said, "The sports page records peoples' accomplishments; the front page nothing but man's failure." Recently, however, scarcely a day has gone by that there hasn't been at least one account in the newspaper sports sections of a high school, university, or professional athlete and even a few coaches running afoul of the law or of league rules regarding drug sales, possession, or use. Indeed, the sports pages of newspapers seem sometimes to have more in them about the travails of athletes with drug problems than about the games being played. For example, the *Los Angeles Times* recently reported that, of 35 weight lifters who had registered for an Ontario lifting competition, 25 withdrew after receiving notification that a drug test would be administered to all entrants. The *Times* never published an account of the competition's results.

It is sad but true. The world of sport is up to its neck in substance abuse.

An Athlete's Choices

Don Schollander, the Olympic swimming champion, has written of two choices facing athletes at the threshold of pain:

> You can back-off...or you can force yourself to drive to the finish....It is right there, at the pain barrier, that the great competitors separate from the rest. Most swimmers back away from the pain! A champion pushes himself on into agony.... When it comes it is oddly satisfying because you know it had to come and now it is there because you are meeting it, taking it without breaking down...because you enjoy the triumph of going through it, knowing it is the only way you can win. If you can push yourself through that pain barrier into real agony, you're a champion.

Shollander's suggested choices, then, are to quit or to push ahead.

But some athletes seem to think that there is a third, which Shollander has neglected to mention — that of striving for championship status without paying the price in agony or hard work. This seems to be the course chosen by many young athletes today in the form of blood-doping, the use of performance-enhancing agents, and even the use of hard, illegal drugs.

There are many prescriptions offered by profit-seekers to make the way "easier" for athletes. To forget pain, one can seek satisfaction by "eating, drinking, and being merry" or turning to drugs. These choices offer escape from the realities of the moment, but they come at a very high price. The price is so staggering, in truth, that it has forced many young athletes into personal bankruptcy.

The Trend

School boards and college administrations everywhere are experiencing the frustrations of dealing with the elusive problem of substance abuse, while enduring the impatience of parents and others who suffer the consequences of the drug craze. It is naturally of concern that the trend may ultimately result in a generation of young people with chemical dependency.

Scott Ostler of the *Los Angeles Times*, despairing of recent revelations concerning drug use by athletes, has facetiously described the future of sports like this:

> We'll see muscle-building drugs, pain-killing drugs, mood-altering drugs, and plain old good-time drugs to make it through another boring lecture in the history of bumper pool. We'll see teenage athletes puffing, popping, shooting, and snorting — in short, building character through chemistry.

Let us hope Ostler is wrong!

The Effects of Drug Use on Athletes

A sad and ironic fact is that many of the substances athletes use to improve their performances do not have the intended effect.

Many substances of no value to athletes have long been thought to be useful. According to Dr. Robert Murphy, team physician at Ohio State University, oxygen on the sidelines is one of these. For the most part, using food supplements, taking multi-vitamins, and carbohydrate-loading — popular among marathoners — are also of no value.

It bears mention in this context that amphetamines do not help improve athletic performance either. Psychologically addicting, they tend to lift the mood, increase aggressiveness and hostility, and make users hyper-active. (I shall not indulge in examples of the many physiological costs of drug use.)

While some drugs thought to be useful are not, some that seem harmless are now known to have negative effects. For example, according to Dr. Murphy, "diuretics which are water pills being used by wrestlers...who try to make weight...set off an electrolyte problem in the body which sometimes can be fatal."

The profound negative effects of other drugs—*e.g.*, heroin—are well-known. We also know that the use of anabolic steroids by athletes in early puberty can result in growth stunting and other problems.

Reasons for Substance Abuse

There are many reasons for the increased incidence of substance abuse among athletes. Knowledge of these reasons would, I feel, help coaches in their efforts to inform students and to influence students against drug involvement.

One factor generally accepted as a cause of greater use is American society's attitude toward drugs. It is almost as though, knowing the difficulties in prosecuting drug cases, the public closes its eyes to the abuses occurring everywhere and grows numb to the problem! Meanwhile, young people are daily exposed to advertisements for drugs to promote sleep, drugs for staying awake, drugs for losing weight, drugs for gaining weight, drugs to relieve pain. We have become so "wrapped up in our freedom that no one wants tough laws," suggests Frank Layden, the general manager and former coach of the Utah Jazz.

A second cause of the increase in substance abuse on the college athletic scene is the pressure to win, which seems to have served as incentive for some athletes to "go the drug route." In professional athletics, where play is the athletes' business and winning promotes their future business, many will go to almost any length to secure their places on rosters.

A third factor contributing to abuses is the widespread publicity about drug use by athletes. This publicity has lent credibility to drug use among younger athletes, who fail to read on about the destruction ultimately being inflicted on the drug users.

A fourth factor responsible for increases in substance abuse centers on the influence of coaches, trainers, and parents. It is now known that, in some instances, coaches and trainers have themselves become directly involved in the intolerable practices of disseminating drugs and knowingly avoiding confrontations with athletes who are drug users. Parents may also share in the blame for drug abuse. When parents, in the conduct of their own lives, freely indulge in drugs for medication or use alcohol and tobacco "to relieve stress," the young are more apt to follow the pattern in their own lives.

Alcohol, Nicotine, and Marijuana

My own sense of the substance abuse problem is that alcohol is at the root of most other drug "happenings." A social and recreational drug obtainable without prescription, alcohol tends to be the substance that introduces youth to the world of drugs. It is the most abused drug among athletes, with about 60 per cent using it regularly.

Too frequently alcohol is excluded from the discussion of drug-related problems, as though it were not a drug about which we ought to be concerned. In reality, alcohol is the drug about which we must be *most* concerned, because it is the one most easily obtained and most widely used. It has been estimated that over 90 per cent of young athletes are exposed to alcohol before the age of fourteen and that serious drinking problems, including adolescent alcoholism, have touched around four million Americans before the age of 18.

Seemingly of less concern than alcoholism itself are other problems that arise from alcohol use: impaired eye-hand coordination, lengthened reaction time, possibly birth defects in children, and so on. Of special interest to athletes are tests that reveal decreases in speed, endurance, strength, and power following alcohol consumption. Also, many medical authorities are suggesting that alcohol, like tobacco, stimulates excessive blood-clotting. At the very least, presence of alcohol in the blood increases blood pressure, needlessly making the heart work harder.

The use of nicotine, especially through tobacco smoking, will over a period of time promote the "coating" of the inner linings of blood vessels, thus narrowing the vessels' opening and increasing blood pressure — and increased blood pressure is known to contribute to heart disease. In the short term, nicotine residue's infiltration of lung tissue often serves to diminish an athlete's ability to sustain a high level of cardiovascular performance.

Smokeless tobacco such as chewing tobacco is known to cause oral carcinomata (cancer). In addition, the chewing of tobacco is a repulsive, habit-forming pastime that frequently leaves baseball dugouts — even those of high-school and college teams — looking and smelling like pigpens.

The NCAA has worked diligently in recent years to identify drugs that are injurious to athletes, and it has even institutionalized drug testing at championship events. Yet the NCAA has not even suggested measures for discouraging the use of smokeless tobacco at its events.

Alcohol and nicotine, among drugs the two biggest drug killers, are legal, and they can be purchased at almost all supermarkets in America. Largely because of their easy accessibility, the likelihood is very high that they will continue to be problem drugs for athletes.

Marijuana and hashish, both illegal, are rapidly becoming as widely used in some high-schools as alcohol. Because of the acceptance of the use of these drugs as a recreational vice, they create problems similar to those caused by alcohol. Marijuana users can expect impairment in perceptual functions, memory loss, and — most tragic — permanent personality change. "[Marijuana] is addictive," according to Ohio State's Dr. Murphy, "and in some individuals terribly addictive."

Steroids and Growth Hormones

Much has been written recently of growth hormones (STH). Athletes, particularly weight lifters, are attracted to STH because of its potential anabolic (muscle-building) effects. Its popularity is based on the belief that it does not have the undesirable side effects (such as growth of facial hair in women and loss of hair in men) of other steroids. STH is costly, however, and procuring money to support the practice of using it has led some to crime.

Much is still unknown about the long-term effects of the use of growth hormones. But many doctors, including Dr. Gertrude Costin, a noted pediatric endocrinologist at the Children's Hospital of Los Angeles, wonder why young athletes are gambling with their health by injecting themselves with it.

The evidence on the effects of anabolic steroids on the human body, like the evidence on the effects of so many other substances, is inconclusive. There is conflicting evidence on whether steroids build strength. But researchers have found that the injected hormones can lead to liver damage, sterility, hair loss, immune system problems, hormone imbalance, and heart disease.

One of the reasons data has been slow in surfacing regarding steroid use is that there are so many different types of steroids. "There are some 80 different anabolic steroids or at least various formulations," according to Russell Oldfield of Specialized Assays, a Nashville testing laboratory. The scarcity of labs qualified to conduct steroid testing and the high cost of testing have compounded the problem.

Concern about steroid usage mounted to new heights in 1985 with the revelation that a university track coach had dispensed prescription drugs to athletes including a runner who had died. The president of the university resigned in the wake of the scandal that followed.

Interestingly, many student athletes involved in the drug counseling programs provided at a few universities speak freely of street drugs but turn into "clams" when questioned about steroids. Because steroids can still be legally procured, some athletes reason that they are "ok" and choose not to be persuaded otherwise. In fact, in almost every city in America, bodybuilding cultists can find doctors who will prescribe these drugs for them.

Bloodpacking

The practice of "bloodpacking" or "blood doping," publicized by the admitted use of some members of the U. S. Olympic cycling team in 1984, involves removing some of one's blood (usually a quart), freezing it, and injecting it back into the body just prior to competing. This procedure increases the oxygen content in the blood, enhancing endurance by about 25 per cent.

Dr. Bob Goldman, author of *Death in the Locker Room*, has warned of the dangers of this practice. "When you handle blood," says Dr. Goldman, "there's always the risk of hepatitis or AIDS [acquired immune deficiency syndrome] if the blood of different athletes gets mixed up." There are also the dangers of infection or clotting — both of which could be very serious.

Drug Use as a Health Issue

In our impatience with the problems of drug use by athletes, coaches must not forget that drug use remains basically a health problem. Whether drugs are legal or illegal, they are potentially harmful to those who use them; the end result of their use is sickness.

The role of the coach in dealing with athletes' drug problems must support the laws controlling the sale of drugs and societal or institutional regulations deterring their use. But coaches, more than any others, must be conscious that their educational responsibilities require full attention to the needs of the students who are troubled with drug habits. The responsibilities include those of providing preventative educational resources for athletes and of remaining compassionate with those who become afflicted.

Many athletes who get sidetracked by substance abuse do in fact recover, and coaches often play an important role in the recovery. The coach's participation in the recovery can be more valuable if the coach fully understands that drug use is, almost always, a remediable health problem.

The Athlete's Image

Sadly, the violation of rules in an effort to increase physical abilities tarnishes the reputations of those athletes who are the true sports heroes. The drug problem has therefore become one more in the long line of issues with which coaches must deal. We cannot allow the cheating of a few to eclipse the fact that most athletes are superbly disciplined, completely honest, in control of themselves, and fully able to resist the temptations that surround them. Coaches must help preserve this "image" of athletics — and to do so, they must be more vigilant of the drug scene, more alert, more knowledgeable, and more understanding than ever before.

21
SEXISM
a slight of the highest order

> Woman's degradation is in man's idea of his sexual rights. Our religion, laws customs, are all founded on the belief that woman was made for man. Come what will, my whole soul rejoices in the truth that I have uttered.
> *Letter to Susan B. Anthony*, Elizabeth Cady Stanton

For some strange reason, human beings have difficulty accepting differences. As soon as people gain sufficient intellect to recognize differences in others, they invariably develop attitudes of suspicion or fear—attitudes that may center on differences in height, weight, physical incapacity, skin color, manner of dress, length of hair, tone of voice, or even gender. Only when we make an educated effort to bring our habits of thought under the rule of reason are we able to overcome such attitudes.

Biases having to do with gender, often referred to as sexism, tend to endure longer than most because there is widespread acceptance of the gender biases built into our patterns of living. And these biases are clearly present in the world of sports, especially to the detriment of women. In fact, the struggles of women athletes on the courts and fields of play have drawn less attention recently than the efforts of these women to challenge the attitude of male privilege and to win the opportunity to play.

Sexism Around Us

Examples of sexism abound, often concealed in subtleties of speech or behavior discerned only by the most sensitive.

One summer, when my family was travelling in New England, we happened upon the nemesis of all summer travellers: road construction. Traffic was backed up for miles, and the sound of air hammers made conversation all but impossible. We alternately opened the car windows to allow air to enter and closed them to shut out the sound and dust.

Periodically there were signs reading,
Caution — Men Working Ahead

My wife, observing the women on the road crews, remarked in her usual matter-of-fact manner on the omission of more appropriate generic language. She was absolutely correct. Things as simple as road signs can reveal mindless disregard for the contributions of womankind, even in the world of road-construction workers.

My mother, an avid "doer" in her teen years, recalls that even the rules of a game she played in childhood reflected sexual subserviency. She has related,

When a boy played the game, he would count off on all the buttons on his garment and say, "When I grow up, I'm going to be a rich man, poor man, beggarman, thief,...,doctor, lawyer, merchant, chief." But when the girls did it, they would chant, "When I grow up I am going to *marry* a rich man, poor man, beggarman, thief,...,doctor, lawyer, merchant, chief."

Sexist thought was alive and vocal on a recent flight I took from Nashville to California. Going through the customary speech of welcome and orientation for passengers, a flight attendant introduced the cabin crew. "Our co-pilot this morning," said the attendant, "is Captain Linda Sullivan." Immediately a passenger bellowed out, "You've got to be joking. I want out of here!" His clear displeasure at the idea of a female co-pilot having control over his safety was apparently more than his ingrained gender biases would allow him to tolerate. I suspect that other, less demonstrative passengers shared the same concerns. Amazing!

In recent years, there has been an outcry from women's groups demanding a halt to the blatant, and not so blatant, biases that continue in our society. Particular attention has been focused on discriminatory living practices and double standards of wages for male and female employees. Many churches are struggling with inclusive language in their liturgy, and governmental organizations are beginning to address similar issues as the level of consciousness is raised concerning discriminatory language practices, and wage scales.

Sexism in Sports

Of course, the reminders are many that sports programs have not been free from bias against women. For decades, denial of sporting opportunities to American women was more often the rule than the exception.

In the eyes of some male coaches, athletics are a male arena. Women's sports, they reason, are sub-activities that should be relegated to smaller budgets, secondary facilities, hand-me-down equipment, *etc*.

My own sister, an exceptional athlete who was constantly told in her youth that "girls don't like to compete," suffered the plight of many young women, being forced to sublimate her athletic energies into channels more acceptable for girls. I was witness to the sexist attitudes in the community in which we grew up. Men organized boys-only "pee-wee" teams; men taught all physical education classes; men coached the interschool teams and organized the high school intramural programs. My sister's only real opportunity to display her athletic skills were during informal neighborhood playground competitions with boys.

Sexism of a similar sort exists today, even at the college level. It is evident, for example, in the student athletic handbook of a prominent, eastern, "coeducational" college, which fields teams in a number of women's sports. The handbook describes the general aims of the athletic program like this:

1. To provide a program of safety for all *men* at the highest priority.
2. To educate *him* in rules, skills, strategies, conditioning and sportsmanship.
3. To help development to *his* highest levels of potential.
4. To provide an enjoyable experience for all participants.

The sexism here does not strike me as an accident of language. It represents, rather, a common attitude of masculine privilege or gross oversight.

According to the *Los Angeles Times*, eleven women graduates of Temple University brought a $1.8 million class-action, sex-discrimination suit against the University in 1988 for unfair practices in athletics. The settlement of the suit brought improved conditions for women's sports at Temple. But much improvement remains to be made at many other educational institutions. In fact, protests continue to mount at many colleges over tactless mistakes or practices unfair to women athletes.

Largely because of media attention, intercollegiate sports have long been the kingdom of the male — and males have not been quick to take a step backwards in behalf of the promotion of women's sports. Too often, women are relegated to practice hours less convenient than men's, to inadequate spaces, and to budgets dwarfed by those afforded men's programs.

Even at the University of Iowa — where Christine Grant, the Primary Women's Administrator, has experienced grand success in women's athletics — the men's budget has remained more than twice that of the women's. As Grant has said,

> There are so many inequities that still exist. For every free education given to a woman, there are two given to the males. In an ideal society, if the population were about 50-50, the same ratio should apply to all sports. It is difficult to accept in an institution where education is the primary goal. I can't conceive that such an institution should afford one sex twice as many opportunities as the other.

Sexism and the Law

In 1972, Congress passed Title IX of the *Education Amendments Act*, which barred sexual discrimination in any educational program receiving federal monetary assistance. Few would deny that Title IX has improved athletic opportunities for women.

Prior to the passage of Title IX, there were on average 2.5 sports for women at American colleges, about 16 percent of the students participating on intercollegiate teams were women, and (according to the U.S. Commission on Civil Rights) women used 2.1 percent of collegiate athletic budgets. By 1980, there were on average 7.3 sports for women at American colleges, 29 percent of the students participating in intercollegiate athletics were women, and women used 14.3 percent of the athletic budgets. By 1988, over 120,000 women were participating in athletic programs at 4 year institutions — about 33 percent of all athletes.

Although these figures point to definite strides in the growth of women's athletics, they do not suggest that parity in sports has been achieved. In fact, it has not.

Some erosion to the progress of women's sports was felt in 1984 due to a ruling by the United States Supreme Court in *Grove City v. Bell*. According to this ruling, the fact that a college received federal monetary assistance did not ensure that Title IX applied to all of the college's athletic programs; the application of Title IX, said the court, was restricted to the specific programs that received the federal money. As a result of this ruling, discriminatory patterns at many colleges and universities were left unchecked.

Following this setback, hope was restored in March 1988 with Congressional passage of the Civil Rights Restoration Act. This action, in effect, overturned the Supreme Court's 1984 decision and restored the governing principles of Title IX. If an institution receives federal funds, all programs within the institution must adhere to the tenets of Title IX. Still, disparities in scholarships and in allotments for travel, housing, and meals are common.

It is a sad fact that, at a few institutions, only the pressure of Title IX has generated any provision for improved facilities and competitive environments for women. Yet, at many institutions athletic facilities provided for women's usage are little more than outdated male structures on which the only change is a "WO" painted in front of the "MEN" on the toilet door.

Women and the NCAA

Many—especially college administrators (and I was one of those)—felt that, when the Association for Intercollegiate Athletics for Women (AIAW) went out of business in 1983 and women's programs were brought under the umbrella of the NCAA, parity would rapidly be achieved. Parity has, however, been elusive.

G. Ann Uhlir, Dean of the College of Health, Physical Education, Recreation, and Dance at Texas Women's University, wrote in the July-August 1987 issue of *Academe* that

> in no area of higher education are women so noticeably absent from the prestigious positions of decision making [as in the administration of athletics]. A woman may even aspire more realistically to become a chief executive officer or a member of a governing board than to become a Director of Athletics of an NCAA Division I institution.

Linda Jean Carpenter, an author from Brooklyn College, supports Uhlir's point:

> In 1972, 90-100% of [women's] athletic programs were headed by females who made all the decisions. Scheduling, budget, personnel, they were in charge of it all. They didn't have to answer to anyone. Now only 16% of women's athletic programs have that level of responsibility

[resting in a woman administrator]...Even those women who are involved are not making the ultimate decisions, as they were in 1972 under the auspices of the AIAW.

It appears, then, that among the major losers in the association of women's' athletics with the NCAA may have been women administrators.

For years, the NCAA supported the rights of women to "try out" for men's teams. This verbalized policy was a "cop out" at providing women's teams with satisfactory sports programs of their own. It also served as protection against litigation. In fact, the policy benefited only the most exceptional women athletes — those who could successfully compete in highly financed men's programs.

Although the policy was ruled unfair by Title IX, the biases that supported it still persist in many male-oriented programs.

Women and Coaching

Today, fewer than 50 percent of the coaches of women's sports teams are women.

I have talked about this with male athletic directors who head up mixed programs, and I have found their responses to be predictable. In many instances, biases against women in sports are made evident by their efforts at misogynistic "humor" — "humor" built on territorial-defensive attitudes towards facilities, budgets, training spaces, practice times, *etc.* Such "humor" reached low levels during and immediately after the over-publicized tennis match between Billie Jean King and Bobby Riggs in 1973 and during the mud wrestling extravaganzas of the early 1980's.

One athletic director offered this simplistic explanation for the paucity of women in coaching: "We can't pay women coaches what they want because their programs don't generate revenue — so, few apply." Unless chief executives and other top administrators exert pressure on program directors, especially in hiring practices, the future of quality female leadership in the coaching and administration of women's sports programs seems bleak.

Where possible, the solid role models provided by women coaching women's teams would be beneficial, if for no other reason than to help dispel the generalized notion that women are not competitive, knowledgeable, or ambitious. In a relationship with a woman coach, young women athletes can discover womanhood and identify with it. Also, women athletes are more apt to openly and usefully discuss women-related health and social concerns with women coaches than with men.

These concerns must be made institutional concerns, and institutional administrators must be made conscious of them.

Attitudes toward Women Athletes

An example of gender bias surfaced in a 1985 court case concerning a high school girl from Ohio. An out-of-court settlement reinstated the girl to the school's football team following the discovery that her principle had told her, "Go home, bake cookies, get pregnant, and have babies like girls are supposed to do."

Attitudes of this sort were more the rule in the nineteenth century, when it was commonly thought that a woman's body, and even her mind, should not be exposed to serious experiences in school — and certainly not in sports. Any form of education, it was felt, was wasted on women, whose roles in life should be those of childbearing and homemaking. Some — including oppressed women — even held to the generalizations that public display of exercise is not feminine — indeed, that it is unhealthy for women to perspire — and that the female personality is not by nature competitive.

Although these attitudes are not voiced as openly these days, they seem to be reviving as a backlash to the strides made in women's sports since the passage of Title IX. Women athletes, say some men, are lesbian, uncoordinated, weak, or worse. Having adopted these attitudes, these men will sometimes admit to their sexual biases and with no apologies. Even some men who coach women's sports are suspect in the attitudes that they bring to their work.

It is the presence of these dispositions and the resulting discrimination toward women athletes that has prompted the rise of radical elements in defense of women's rights. Many of those involved in the women's movement feel that, to counter exclusivity, the power of numbers must be employed.

Women in the Olympics

Historically, the International Olympic Committee has been slow in fully considering women's interests in competition. In the 1984 Los Angeles Games, men's events outnumbered women's by five in track and field alone. The 3000 meter run and the marathon were first-ever events for women in the

1984 program, and both were resisted by Olympic moguls. Not until the American Civil Liberties Union brought suit and threatened adverse publicity to the Games did Olympic officials act. Then one Olympic official, in an effort to absolve the Olympic Committee of blame in the delay of a decision, had the audacity to say this:

> Another innovation I really like is that we've added to women's sports in these Games...without being asked.

Nonsense! Continued resistance to the addition of the 5000 and 10,000 meter runs for women was met in the preparations for the 1988 Games in Seoul, Korea, with only the 10,000 ultimately entered into the events program for women.

Interestingly, media coverage of the 1984 Olympics, which heavily featured men's events, seized upon the "cutsie" aspects of Mary Lou Retton's performances, on the Zola Budd/Mary Decker collision in the 3000 meter run, and on Gabriele Anderson-Schiess' grotesque stagger at the finish of the marathon as the highlights of the women's Olympic activities. Comparatively little attention was given to brilliant accomplishments by other women in competition, particularly in field hockey and in the equestrian events.

Sexism and the Media

When and where they can, coaches need to educate the media on the truths about women in sports. In some areas of America, young girls avoid athletic participation because their parents — led by the media's disproportionate attention to boy's sports-come to believe that athletic participation is less vital or appropriate for girls — steer their daughters away from sports toward more "feminine" activities like cheerleading.

In Maine, a short article on a girls' softball game described one team's shortstop as a real "tomboy" who "threw the ball like Robin Yount." This kind of journalism only reinforces the misconception that sports are a male domain.

In another example of poor journalistic taste, a reporter asked the star center of a university's basketball team who had just broken the school's scoring record if she would agree to pose in a bubble bath! How much more healthy it would be if female athletes could get into sports without societal encumbrances having to do with appearance, attire, behavior patterns, or sex.

✻ ✻ ✻ ✻ ✻

I have relished the occasions when I could watch my daughter express herself as an intercollegiate athlete of note in squash racquets and field hockey. But, today I lament the threat, created by governmental and institutional laxity toward enforcement of equal rights, to my granddaughter's opportunity for an equal chance to express herself through sports.

If any disagree with what I have said about sexism, I suggest that they ask themselves whether their own daughters, sisters, granddaughters, or nieces should have to search in vain, as many have done before them, for the same opportunities as those provided their brothers. How can anyone claiming to be an educator justifiably exclude people from athletics or reduce their opportunities solely because of their gender?

Sexism, alive even today, only serves as a hindrance to real progress in the growth of sports and of competitive opportunities for all.

140 OFF THE BENCH

22
RACISM
a disastrous disease for sport

[My faith] keeps me from judging any man by the color of his skin. It teaches me to judge him by his deeds and his conscious behavior. And it teaches me to be for the rights of all human beings.

Malcolm X

I recall with clarity a spring day in 1954. As our college baseball team travelled to a game in a nearby Ohio town, we heard on the car radio that the Supreme Court had handed down a landmark civil rights ruling which in effect outlawed segregation. Following the game our group, which included a black catcher, was refused service at a roadside diner.

Thirty years later, at the 1984 convention of the National Association of Basketball Coaches in Seattle, a prominent coach and athletic director boasted in informal conversation that his program was free from racism. "In fact," he noted, "I hired a black assistant a year ago." A colleague added that through college sport "we've paved the way for human justice in this country." Idle boasting, at best!

The coaching profession has indeed taken some progressive strides in correcting the "ism"-attitudes in sports. In recent times, there has been a greater consciousness of words and deeds with racist implications. But I am not alone in judging that we still have considerable room for improvement. Few days pass during which subtle acts or statements reflecting racist biases do not occur within the ranks of coaches. The "isms" are alive and flourishing. Residual feelings of bigotry live on, often surfacing in generalized statements of prejudice or in unfair practices.

Generalizations and Attitudes toward Race

Nowadays the ways of racism are often subtle, sometimes couched in euphemisms and almost always based on generalizations. But, like sore pimples, racist attitudes eventually rise to the surface and hurt somebody.

Should coaches find that racist feelings exist in their own hearts and minds, they must cleanse themselves somehow if they are to be effective in their work. Generalizations that paint pictures of people based on skin color or other physical features foster racist attitudes that can be deleterious to coaches — especially those whose daily toils center on relationships with athletes from a multitude of backgrounds.

As is the case in many areas of a coach's working regimen, the habit of formulating attitudes based on hearsay, rumor, or perceptions derived from others' biases or one's own limited experience inhibits impartial judgement. Sadly, coaching policies, procedures, and practices often emanate from such attitudes.

The problem with this pattern of decision-making is that it lacks objectivity and is therefore incompetent. To avoid incompetence, the professional coach must fervently strive to be objective — especially in matters of ethnic sensitivity — by adopting an open-minded, fact-finding approach in dealings with athletes. Anything less sets a course vulnerable to charges of racial inconsideration, or worse.

Racism and Genetics

In crass examples of generalized, prejudicial statements, Al Campanis, the former General Manager of the Los Angeles Dodgers, and Jimmy "The Greek" Snyder, a television sports analyst, revealed in comments aired to millions of television viewers what many coaches believe — that blacks dominate many of the team sports because of genetically favorable physical attributes. Small wonder that some big-time football and basketball coaches focus their recruiting almost entirely on black prospects!

Richard E. Lapchick, Director of the Center for the Study of Sports in Society at Northeastern University points out that, since the 1936 Olympic games which featured the triumphs of Jesse Owens, "people have been obsessed" with the notion that Owens' success was due to basic "physical differences between blacks and whites." And Lapchick notes other ethnic generalizations in sports. "When Jewish players dominated basketball in the

1920's and 30's," he writes, "writers discussed mentality, not muscle development." Lapchick cites a 1933 article by variety show host and sports columnist Ed Sullivan, in which Sullivan wrote,

> Nat Holman, Jewish star of the Celtics is a marvelous player. He has always reminded me of Benny Leonard. Both are of the same alertness....Jewish players seem to take naturally to the game. Perhaps this is because the Jew is a natural gambler and will take chances. Perhaps it is because he devotes himself more closely to a problem than others will.

And Lapchick finds similar attitudes in the writings of Dean Cromwell, who coached the 1936 American Olympic team. Wrote Cromwell,

> The Negro excels in the events he does because he is closer to the primitive than the white man. It was not that long ago that his ability to spring and jump was a life and death matter to him.

As recently as 1971, an article in *Sports Illustrated* suggested that, because of superior tendon development, black athletes are advantaged in "double jointedness." Sounding a little like Al Campanis in 1988, the article's author added that "perhaps because of a physical inheritance, no black has ever been a swimming champion." (Lapchick reports that Bill Russell of Celtic basketball fame had this retort to the *Sports Illustrated* article: "All that the racial upheaval of the 1960's had taught *Sports Illustrated* was that it's OK to be a racist as long as you try to sound like a doctor.")

A 1989 NBC documentary featuring a physiologist and an anthropologist attempted to demonstrate that blacks are better athletes than whites. In my judgement, the program proved little except that cultural and environmental factors more reasonably explain performance differences in various sports than variance in physiological make-up.

In almost any sports journal or broadcast these days, a discerning listener can pick up a number of racial slurs. Most, I'm certain, are unintended — but unintended slurs are slurs nonetheless. For example, in the constant litany of references to successful white athletes, mention is more often made to attributes of mind — such as determination, cleverness, or mental quickness — than to natural athletic ability or physical quickness. Mention of such physical attributes tend to be reserved for explanations of the successes of Latin or black athletes.

Minorities in Professional Sports and Coaching Roles

The inclusion of black and Latin athletes in professional sports did not begin to occur until after World War II. It was years later that a minority presence was realized with any regularity.

Professional football excluded non-white athletes until Kenny Washington was recruited by the Los Angeles Rams in 1946. Jackie Robinson broke racial barriers in baseball the following spring. Blacks were excluded from pro basketball until 1950 when Chuck Cooper joined the Boston Celtics and "Sweetwater" Clifton joined the New York Knicks. It was another twenty years before Alabama, one of college football's perennial powers under legendary Coach "Bear" Bryant, recruited its first black player.

In coaching and in sports administration, opportunities for those from racial minorities continue to be limited. Peter Ueberoth, who retired as Commissioner of Major League Baseball in 1989, repeatedly pointed to the paucity of the minority presence in administrative positions in professional baseball as a matter that owners must address.

Opportunities may also be limited on the field for black athletes. In an article entitled "Blacks in Sports" that appeared in an Ohio State University student newspaper, James Leickly quotes Robert Jiobu and Timothy Curry, associate professors of Sociology, on the function of "stacking" as a form of subtle racism in athletics. Stacking is the practice of placing athletes at certain positions based on their ethnic "abilities." "Few blacks play quarterback, center, or middle linebacker in football," they point out, even though blacks comprise about half the roster slots in professional football. In baseball the practice applies to pitchers, catchers, and the infield positions. "Blacks are apt to play the peripheral positions, away from the decisions of play, such as running back, wide receiver, defensive back or outfielder", say the sociologists. Stacking, of course, can also hurt a white player seeking a position considered best suited to non-white athletes.

Although there are now a plethora of television commercials featuring black athletes, there remains a considerable gap between the endorsement opportunities for black stars and those for whites. Only some of the truly great black professional athletes, like Michael Jordan, fare as well as their white brothers and sisters in the profitable enterprise of advertising. Dr. William H. Edwards, a highly respected black sports sociologist, has suggested that the imbalance is another example of the exploitation of the educationally disadvantaged and of those from racial minorities.

The absence of minority presence is pronounced at all levels, but educational institutions, particularly, are remiss in placing minority coaches. Tony Yates — an All-American basketball player at Cincinnati University during the school's NCAA championship years — was considered by members of the coaching circle to be one of the best teachers of defensive basketball. Yet Yates, who is black, served as an assistant basketball coach at various universities for twenty years and did not receive a head coaching opportunity until 1983.

In December, 1989, the NCAA News reported that 36 percent of university football players but only 4.3 percent of head coaches are black. "Most Division I schools have never even interviewed a black candidate for a head coaching job in basketball or football," wrote sociologist Edwards. "Beyond basketball and football, it's an utter wasteland. College baseball is dismal. There's not a single black head coach in Division I."

Unfortunately, colleges have not been required to answer for their poor hiring records in athletics in the way that professional sport has been in recent years.

The Coach's Role

The presence of athletes of various minority backgrounds is commonplace on most campuses today. Coaches should use all their skill and power to challenge any statement or action unfair to these athletes, dealing forthrightly with any words or behaviors that may destroy the feeling of community on their athletic teams. There can be no untroubled hearts for those who, knowingly or otherwise, raise their own stature by oppressing others of different colors or beliefs.

How often ethnic humor is used as a put down or as a tool to isolate the styles of particular athletes! People may laugh at such humor, but the people at whom it is aimed often experience anguish. Coaches rely heavily on humor in their work — at times, they need to in order to preserve their sanity. But humor that reflects on a person's ethnicity serves no useful purpose and can often be destructive to relationships. Even the use of generalized phrases — like "black sheep", "dumb Pole," and "tight as a Tel Aviv merchant" — in describing appearances, attributes, and styles can be equally injurious.

Being well educated and possessing better than average resources, coaches are in a grand position to make a difference in people's attitudes about race. They have no right to hide from the responsibility of making certain that young minds do not foster feelings of superiority over others who appear different. Because of the power of its impact, the profession of coaching has important obligations to the community, the country, and the world to lead the fight against racism.

Coaches are capable of amazing feats but, as they mature to the sensitivities of racism, they must recognize that they cannot make it alone in their work life. As much as any other people, coaches need constantly to re-appraise their attitudes about people. They cannot allow personal biases so to direct their judgements that the lives of others are adversely affected.

Racism as Hatred

Hatred, the product of prejudicial thought, is a sickness as injurious to the human personality as compulsive gambling or alcoholism. It also damages the spirit. It bruises human intellectual potential. It lessens self-esteem. It is both exploitative and manipulative. It kills with words, looks, and lies. Magnified, it leads to big governments taking land from little governments, wealthy overlords using hungry peasants to grow coffee for export to the rich, and power brokers killing those who would challenge their power. Hatred may well be the devil in all of us.

History reveals that the power of hatred is very real — that hatred can devastate and destroy beyond our ability to comprehend. A school counselor friend of mine has tabbed hatred the curse most responsible for racial strife. He elaborated, "White racism has been a part of American life and institutions for a long time, and we are just now beginning to grasp the full extent of the hostility, violence, and treachery that it has wrought in our society. Hatred only recreates hatred."

I recently attended a dinner of international students at a dining hall on our campus. At each table were helium-filled balloons attached by strings to small paper boxes with flags painted on them. The Japanese girl seated next to me picked nervously at one of the paper boxes, breaking away small pieces. Finally the balloon tied to the box lifted off the table and floated to the ceiling. Believing that there must be some symbolic meaning to what had happened, she made the interesting suggestion that, if more of us could shed the burdens of mistrust, disrespect, and prejudice, our spirits too might be lifted in our dealings with people.

Being Positive

A coaching colleague recently told me that he was having problems with a very talented young black basketball player, whom he was not playing because the lad "couldn't conform to the system." Keeping the athlete on the bench, reasoned the coach, was just punishment for his failure to conform. I'm sure many coaches have had similar experiences. I know I have.

I would suggest that, in their relationships with "testy" athletes, coaches strive to discover the truth that punitive action sometimes can drive the wedge of separation between coaches and athletes even deeper. We need to learn ways to say "yes" to students with different "styles," because it is this "yes" that helps to reconcile people and to reinforce their relationship. It is, I admit, easier to be negative in our responses than positive, easier also to criticize than to praise. But a conscious effort to swallow some displeasures with an "ethnic style" may serve the greater good by establishing a rapport and that will earn for coaches the respect needed to achieve larger aims.

❋ ❋ ❋ ❋ ❋

The beauty in most young people is that they haven't had the years to gather the nasty attitudes of some adults. Racial biases are less a part of their makeup.

I recently read of a ten-year old boy who had written an autobiographical theme for his class based on a story he had read about Dr. Martin Luther King, Jr. The fifth grader wrote, "Martin was a man like me. He had all kinds of ideas. They didn't all work. He started lots of things he didn't finish. He was against violence. That is a good idea. He also was good at talking. I am too."

This is a child's rather disarming description of Martin Luther King and his assessment of himself as a person with talent, too. Wouldn't it be wonderful if we could all retain this kind of youthful innocence in our attitudes toward others as we grow older? This can happen only through a positive effort to objectively address the biases we all carry and to shelve them in the interest of competent judgement and effective leadership.

23
THE TEACHING OF VALUES
a coaching concern

> The hope of free man in a frightened world is the values which man puts ahead of inventions when his back is to the wall. These values are beauty, truth, goodness and having a faith, all of which are bomb-proof.
>
> Ralph W. Sockman

As previously emphasized, the modern coach can play a vital role in helping students to discover values that can lead to richer, more meaningful lives. The help may come in the form of personal counsel, interpretations of rules, reprimands, or simply conversations with students about right and wrong conduct in various aspects of their lives.

The Importance of the Teaching of Values

There are coaches who would persuade us that teaching of values—the traits of character and behavior that lend purpose to life — is not important for coaches. Some cite demands on time and some, lack of interest. Others even go so far as to suggest that athletes who concern themselves with values lack toughness or other ingredients necessary for athletic success. In fact, a coaching acquaintance once bragged to me that, after a young man had solicited his counsel on a pressing values question, he had responded thusly: "What the hell do I look like, a priest?"

The truth is, however, that one cannot over-emphasize the importance of a coach's charting a course that includes instruction in values. The responses that coaches seek from athletes are those that will serve the athletes in a creative way throughout their lives. It is desirable, for example, that athletes be dutiful and responsive, yet they are often selfish and rebellious. It is desirable that they be caring of one another, yet they frequently bicker and sulk when their own wishes are not realized. It is desirable that they be loyal and honest, yet they are often critical of coaches and teammates — so preoccupied with their own cravings that they use others and demand unfairly of them. Clearly our work in the teaching of values is ever before us.

As coaches, we can have the sense that we are rendering service to others, that we are enriching human life, that we are upholding values. Because we have this sense, we know that we are contributing something significant to impressionable young people.

The Coach's Special Opportunity

Coaches, more than others in education, have opportunities for teaching values. Almost constantly, in the faces of those with whom coaches work is written the message "Help me!"

Coaches should try to remember that behind each student face lies a potentially beautiful but complex personality with great intrinsic value. It is a pity if coaches see athletes only as tools for gaining personal glory and fail to reach for more substantial goals. And it is even worse if, in their selfishness, coaches try to generate loyalty and enthusiasm from teams by feeding them "perks and frills" rather than wisdom, love, and counsel.

Students often have a remarkable capacity for goodness, but they are also capable of selfish, character-weakening behavior. The opportunities to address these problems are far greater for coaches than for professionals in other fields if, for no other reason, than that the circumstances in which coaches work with students offer phenomenal opportunities to present examples of meaningful responses.

I recall years ago travelling with an aging Spanish cleric through the small mountain hamlets of Ecuador. The priest carried Bibles for distribution, and I carried a bag of assorted balls with which to demonstrate and play. The priest marveled at how much more attentive the children were to the discussions of play than to the instructions on how to pray. With such attention directed toward coaches, it is a shame that we sometimes fall short in providing values lessons as well as lessons in sports.

In his book *Future Shock*, Alvin Toffler wrote,

> The United States is a nation in which tens of thousands of young people flee reality by opting for drug-induced lassitude...in which millions of

THE TEACHING OF VALUES 151

their parents retreat into video-induced stupor or alcoholic haze;...in which legions of elderly vegetate and die in loneliness; in which the flight from family and occupational responsibility has become an exodus; in which masses tame their raging anxieties with Miltown, Librium, Equavil or a score of other tranquilizers and psychic pacifiers.

The playwright Ionesco has called this retreat from reality *rhinoceritis*. In his play *Rhinoceros*, people forget all human values, reason, respect, decency, and become masses of cruel, uncaring, beastial creatures.

These tendencies must be countered, and coaches are in position to do it. The profession of coaching offers the setting of the swim pool, the play field, or the weight room in which the problems of young people often surface and come within reach. And coaches are the most suited of today's adult society to hold the attention of young people and draw their respect. The doors of opportunity through which coaches can enter and serve athletic youth are constantly ajar.

Values at Work

In our generation, one cannot ignore the impact that Dr. Martin Luther King, Jr. has had on values education. His moral leadership was established at the start of his rise to eminence. In 1955, following the arrest of Rosa Parks in Montgomery, Alabama, for refusing to give up her seat in a bus to a white man, Dr. King began to touch the American conscience. At that time he challenged fellow blacks by saying,

> If you will protest courageously, and yet with dignity and love, when the history books are written in future generations, the historians will have to pause and say, There lived a great people...a black people...who injected meaning and dignity into the veins of civilization. This is our challenge and our overwhelming responsibility.

As time passed, King came under great pressure to condone violence, but he rejected the notion out of hand, saying, "If every Negro in the United States turns to violence, I will choose to be that one lone voice preaching that this is the wrong way."

At the time most of the white community of educators stood voiceless and inactive in the struggle for racial justice. From a Birmingham jail, King wrote of this lack of support, "We will have to repent in this generation not merely for the hateful words and actions of the bad people but for the appalling silences of the good people."

Reflecting on those times, one cannot fail to respect King's wisdom and courage. More importantly, if we hold true to the values he espoused then, how vital it is for us to stand and be counted in our efforts to teach those values today!

An example of values at work occurred when Anwar Sadat, President of Egypt, went on a unilateral mission of conciliation and peace to Jerusalem. Sadat and Golda Meier, the Israeli Prime Minister, met and talked with one another even though, only a few years earlier, they had been directing the slaughter of each other's children and grandchildren.

In greeting her former arch-enemy, Meier reminded Sadat how he used to refer to her as "that mean old lady." Later in their conversation, she handed Sadat a package that she had been holding in her lap. "I understand that your first grandchild was born just the other day," Meier said to Sadat. "I've been a grandmother for many years. I have a little gift for your grandchild." As Sadat reached to receive the gift, his chin trembled visibly. It was a touching moment — one with a message for all of us who care about young lives.

If coaches, too, feel that young people are the salt of the earth, we must search for ways to make life more palatable for them. We must help them discover real values that will bring peace and richness to their lives. In coaching, the opportunities are constantly before us to do just that.

Teaching by Example

When coaches fall short professionally by failing to talk to students about matters of values, it is sometimes because their own level of confidence, based on the knowledge of improprieties in their own lives makes them incapable of dealing with those issues. It is obviously difficult to be committed to the teaching of values while being neglectful of values-oriented practices in our own lives.

Some of the more tragic situations I have encountered in years of observing coaches at work are cases in which a coach, trying to be all things to all constituents, has failed to establish a pattern of living to which athletes can look as a model. In values teaching, coaches must strive to be themselves. Only through commitments to values suitable to themselves can they define themselves honestly and establish direction to the job of helping others.

For a coach to come to grips with the topic of values at all requires a commitment to a style of life that allows the discussion of values to surface

THE TEACHING OF VALUES 153

without the appearance of hypocrisy. Choosing such a style of life can be hard for some, but only by making this choice can a coach become free to work with students in matters of such personal import.

Dr. George A. Buttrick, the noted theologian, once said this about the way people in various professions see and interpret life:

> [S]ome businessmen see nothing but...price lists, profits, sales; while others see...the faces of those who work for them, the faces of those who have no work. Some statesmen see nothing but...battleships, voting booths, headlines. Other statesmen see...the faces of the poor, of little children, of those slain in war.

Buttrick could well have included the coaching profession on the list. Some coaches see nothing but wins, automobiles, packed arenas; others see the faces of those engaged in competition, the faces of those who don't get to play, the faces of those agonized by pain or defeat.

Far too many coaches become magnetized to the dollars-and-cents aspect of coaching. Far too many get caught up, sometimes unknowingly, in the rat race to win. But, as William Sloane Coffin once pointed out, "winning a rat race doesn't make the winner any less a rat." Caught up in the race, coaches often forget the deep purposes of their vocation: to teach, lead, and inspire young people to grow to their fullest — physically, socially, emotionally, and even spiritually. This, it would seem, should be the credo of all educators.

It seems to me especially important for those coaching teenagers to reflect on their own lives and the way in which they live them. Reflect, if we can, on our own adolescence and on those who had relationships with us. Think of occurrences in our lives that have molded our ideas. Ponder also the central themes of our adulthood relative to matters of trust, loyalty, honesty, and decency. Are we committed to these things in our own lives? Are we committed to helping others identify and grasp them? These are vital questions for coaches as we inspect our roles in the teaching of young athletes.

Inner Conflicts

It sometimes seems that there is a battle of competing values going on inside each of us. In one corner a voice cries out, "Sacrifice, choose, make painful decisions, take the right path." And in the other corner, glowing like so many neon signs around us, is the advice, "Take it easy, eat your fill, take a pill, take a short-cut."

Many coaches seem to <u>sense conflict in their roles as teachers of values</u>. I see it in their lives and feel it in my own. The conflict centers on the <u>dilemma of winning</u>. The more we win or advance ourselves professionally, the more we want other gratifications, the more exotic our tastes become. Coaches need to <u>guard against becoming so ambitious that they clutter their schedules and confuse themselves with too many demands on their time.</u>

Daniel Yankelovich, a social psychologist, has cautioned that the suppression of desires is often helpful if one is to avoid "becoming a blob of contradictions." What Yankelovich is suggesting, in fact, is that we simplify our lives, freeing time for defining values and for assisting others by sharing ideas with them.

A few coaches are in conflict in a way not connected with time or winning. These coaches see themselves as incapable of working with athletes in the context of teaching values.

It is easy to become disheartened, to lose confidence because of mistakes we have made in our dealings with young athletes. Some coaches even become so disheartened that they leave the profession. These departures — especially by young, educated coaches who try to represent athletes in a positive way — are often a severe loss to the coaching profession.

My suggestion is that coaches who become dissatisfied or disenchanted because of set-backs take heart and give coaching a further try. Imagine the pain of Oklahoma's Barry Switzer, who resigned his football coaching duties disgraced by the many misdemeanors perpetrated by members of his football team! But the profession of coaching needs the talent of Barry Switzer — not the Switzer whose indifference to values learning led to his difficulties, but the Switzer who has learned from the experience.

Looking back on his career, a retired coaching colleague expressed the apprehensions of many as they start out in the profession:

> When I started coaching I felt inadequate to the task but I loved the kids. I have loved more than I have been loved, trusted more than I have been trusted, but the rewards have been mine.

There is something about coaches who give without holding back that yields satisfaction for the giver and great lessons of value for students fortunate enough to have worked with them.

Ray Meyer, the retired coach of the DePaul basketball team, won numerous games in his decades of coaching. But his legacy to the sport he loved was a gift of selfless devotion to the young people with whom he worked. He ever tried to reach beneath the faces to lend values training to the daily coaching regimen.

✼ ✼ ✼ ✼ ✼

It is said that John Hancock wrote his signature large on the Declaration of Independence because he wanted to be certain that King George would see it. Hancock knew about commitment to a purpose, and he was willing to put his life on the line for what he believed. Coaches, too, need that kind of courage and determination as they place instruction in values into their daily schedules.